# North of Naples, South of Rome

# North of Naples, South of Rome

### PAOLO TULLIO

*With illustrations by*
*Susan Morley*

ST. MARTIN'S PRESS ❧ NEW YORK

A THOMAS DUNNE BOOK.
An imprint of St. Martin's Press.

NORTH OF NAPLES, SOUTH OF ROME. Copyright ©
1994 by Paolo Tullio. Illustrations copyright ©
1994 by Susan Morley. All rights reserved. Printed
in the United States of America. No part of this
book may be used or reproduced in any manner
whatsoever without written permission except in
the case of brief quotations embodied in critical
articles or reviews. For information, address
St. Martin's Press, 175 Fifth Avenue,
New York, N.Y. 10010.

ISBN 0-312-19307-6

First published in Great Britain by The Lilliput
Press Ltd., in association with Hamish
Hamilton Ltd.

First U.S. Edition: October 1998

10 9 8 7 6 5 4 3 2 1

To Chris and Diane


Thanks to John and Isabella for their encouragement,
Paul and Kathy for keeping me mobile,
and my wife for being there

# Contents

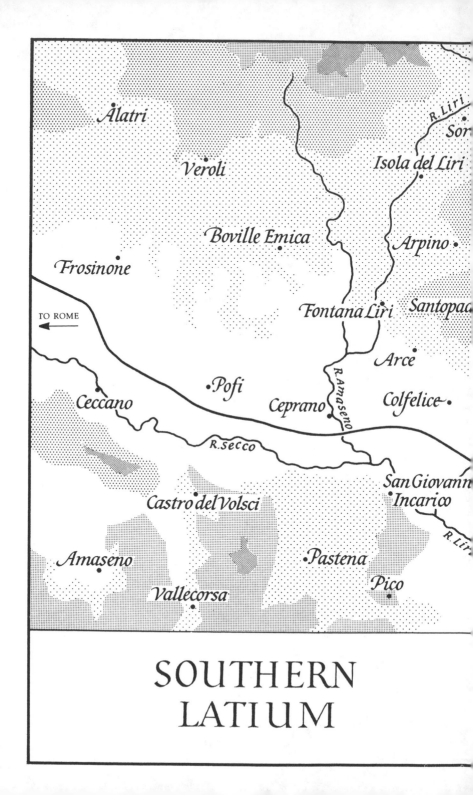

Alatri

Veroli

Isola del Liri

R. Liri

Sor

Boville Emica

Arpino

Frosinone

TO ROME

Fontana Liri

Santopac

Arce

Pofi

Ceccano

Ceprano

Colfelice

R. Amaseno

R. secco

San Giovann
Incarico

Castro del Volsci

R. Lir

Amaseno

Pastena

Pico

Vallecorsa

# SOUTHERN
# LATIUM

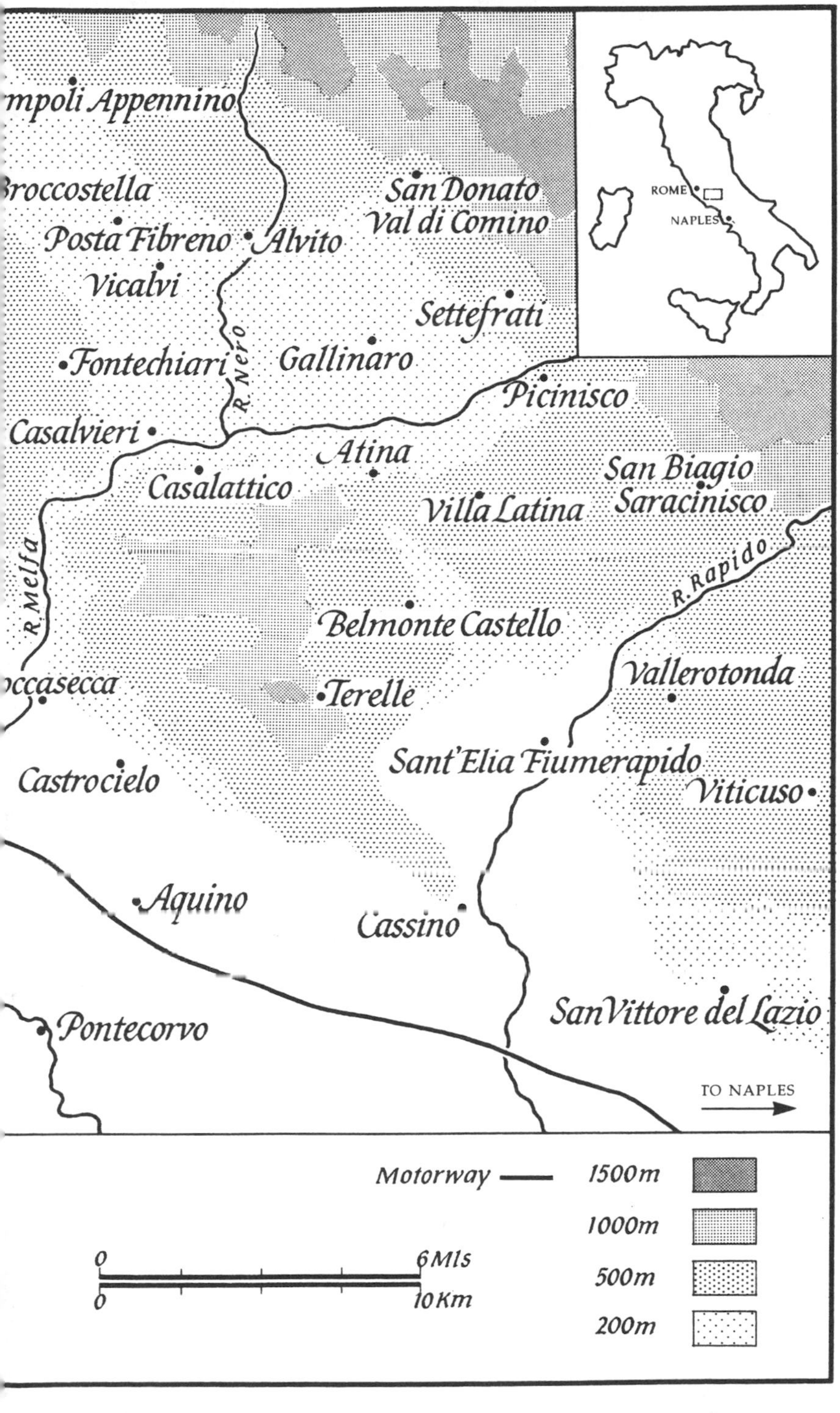

ROME
NAPLES

mpoli Appennino
Broccostella
Posta Fibreno •Alvito
Vicalvi
•Fontechiari
Casalvieri •
Casalattico
R. Melfa
ccasecca
Castrocielo
•Aquino
•Pontecorvo

R. Nero

San Donato
Val di Comino

Settefrati

Gallinaro

Picinisco

Atina

Villa Latina

San Biagio
Saracinisco

R. Rapido

Belmonte Castello

Terelle

Vallerotonda

Sant'Elia Fiumerapido

Viticuso •

Cassino

San Vittore del Lazio

TO NAPLES

Motorway ———    1500m
                1000m
                500m
                200m

0                    6 Mls
0                    10 Km

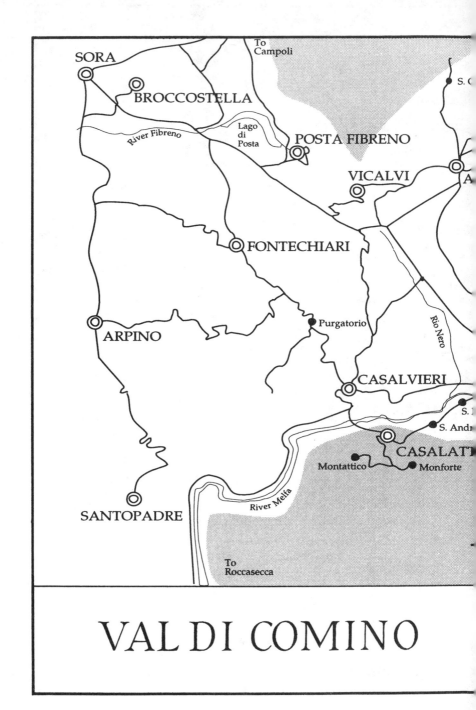

SORA

BROCCOSTELLA

To Campoli

S. C

River Fibreno

Lago di Posta

POSTA FIBRENO

VICALVI

A

FONTECHIARI

Purgatorio

ARPINO

Rio Nero

CASALVIERI

S.

S. Andr

CASALAT

Montattico   Monforte

SANTOPADRE

River Melfa

To Roccasecca

# VAL DI COMINO

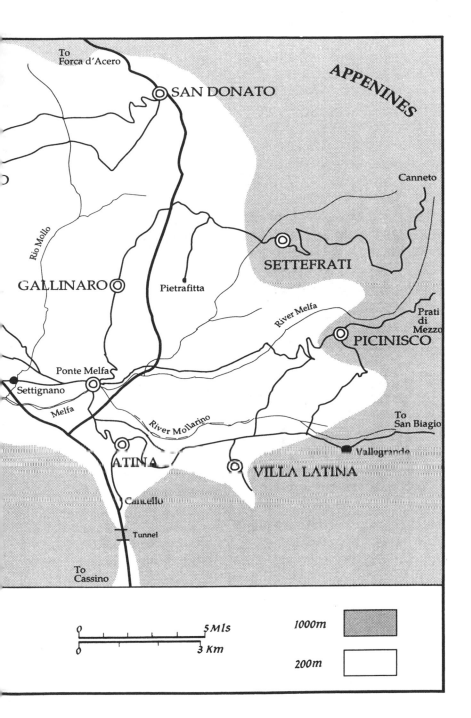

To
Forca d'Acero

SAN DONATO

APPENINES

Canneto

Rio Mollo

SETTEFRATI

GALLINARO

Pietrafitta

River Melfa

Prati
di
Mezzo

PICINISCO

Ponte Melfa

Settignano

Melfa

River Mollarino

To
San Biagio

Vallegrande

ATINA

VILLA LATINA

Cancello

Tunnel

To
Cassino

0                    5 Mls

0                    3 Km

1000m

200m

This is not a book about Italy; it is about the Comino Valley in Lazio. The valley is, none the less, inhabited by Italians who have a lot in common with those who live outside the valley. In fact, they have so much in common that it is tempting to assume that all of Italy works in much the same way as the valley does.

It is a big valley – nearly a fifth of the province of Frosinone. A man could spend much of a lifetime discovering what is worth knowing about its dozen towns. It is big enough to be a world in itself; a simple man could find all he needs within it.

There is no escaping the fact that my viewpoint is provincial, and when the focus is on Gallinaro, my home town, it becomes distinctly parochial. Still, this valley is my Italy; I know it well, and am related to a huge number of its inhabitants. Historically, this was not a rich world; predominantly agricultural, its wealth has always been wine and oil. Unlike Tuscany, the valley contains no large reservoirs of art or culture, it has no beaches, no cathedrals and no tourists. Until recently, large numbers of its inhabitants emigrated to Europe, the Americas and the Antipodes. No one ever came here, they just left.

Lurking within this undisturbed territory is, of course, the real Italy. People from all over the peninsula lay claim to living in the real Italy, but they are wrong. The real Italy lies here, in the Comino Valley, north of Naples, south of Rome, high in the mountains, surrounded by the Apennine peaks.

# Preface

My father was born in 1918 in Gallinaro, one of the twelve villages in the Comino Valley. His father, Luigi, had the dubious distinction of being one of the last soldiers to be killed in the First World War – wounded on 10 November 1918 and dying three days later, six months before my father was born. My grandmother Luisa, young and pretty, refused two offers of marriage and brought up my father and his elder brother by herself. Luigi left her a large house in Gallinaro, which she converted into a petrol station, a bar and a grocery shop. The house is at the bottom of the hill on which Gallinaro stands and on what was then the main road across the valley, so the business prospered.

My father was a good student and won a scholarship at the age of seven to Frascati College, in the Alban Hills, to the south of Rome. It was a boarding school, where the students had only the summer holidays to spend at home. Here he excelled at Latin and Greek, but a year before his baccalaureate he was expelled for bringing a girl to his rooms when it was discovered, despite his protestations, that she was not in fact his cousin. This was a serious blow, since he now had to find a new school with only a year until his university entrance. After nearly ten years at Frascati, he attended his last year of high school at the Tulliano, the classical *lycée* in Arpino, an old city just beyond the confines of the Comino Valley.

Luisa, my father's mother, was not from Gallinaro originally. She came from the village of Casalattico, another of the villages in the valley. Her family, the Fuscos, were farmers in the hamlet of San Nazario. Since the middle of the last century pieces of the farm had been sold off bit by bit – family history has it that this was to cover gambling debts. As it grew smaller, it was no longer able to support the two large families that then worked it. By the turn of the century two brothers, Benedetto and Francesco, had divided the house, and each brother had seven children. Luisa, my grandmother, was the youngest child of the elder brother.

Mario, the eldest child of the younger brother and Luisa's cousin, decided that prospects on the farm were far from good and so he emigrated with two of his brothers to Scotland, but not before the three brothers had married the three Magliocco sisters. Mario had two daughters, the elder of whom, Irene, he sent to school in Italy, where she lived with her aunt Rosa in Casalattico. After returning to Scotland for two years, Irene went back to Italy to the College of Santa Giovanna, in Arpino, where she met my father, Dionisio, her second cousin.

Nuns, being what they are, ensured that contacts between their female charges and the outside world were as short and as sporadic as possible, so it was not until my mother and father were visiting their respective halves of the family house in San Nazario that their romance blossomed. But then came the war. My mother returned to Scotland, while my father studied law at the University of Florence. They corresponded as frequently as they could, but towards the end of the war messages became harder to send. Its last years found my father as a second lieutenant in the Italian army, hiding from the Germans in the mountains surrounding the Comino Valley. The house in San Nazario had been taken over by the Germans as a billet, while a house my father had inherited in Gallinaro was also requisitioned. The Comino Valley was for eighteen months part of the Gustav line holding Cassino, so the density of German troops in it was high.

When Cassino finally fell, the Germans left the valley and the rebuilding began. In Italy it is traditional on New Year's Eve to set off bangers and fireworks. My father told me that New Year's Eve 1944 was quite a sight. All around the valley people had collected the detritus of war and saved it for the celebrations. The sky was alight with tracer bullets, machine guns fired, grenades exploded and high above Casalattico someone pounded the sky with a howitzer. For years afterwards, my great-aunt had a stack of explosives – little cakes about the size of a bar of soap with a hole in the middle, presumably for a detonator. She used them for firelighters. That year everyone in the valley was well armed. The new government was nervous of the strength of the former resistance fighters. My father and his cousin Dino were armed by the government and given a small arsenal to distribute to trusted friends and relations if the expected rebellion ever happened. In 1946 my father was elected mayor of Casalattico, the youngest ever and almost certainly the first with a degree.

In Scotland in 1947 my mother was making preparations to marry a nature-cure practitioner. Shortly before the wedding date my grandfather took her to Italy to visit their relations, since the war had disrupted communications between them for six years. Naturally, while in Casalattico, my mother met my father again and their romance started anew. On her return to Scotland the impending marriage to the Scot was called off with three weeks to go, gifts were returned and a new wedding planned. Shortly afterwards my father, disillusioned with post-war Italy, came to Scotland to marry my mother. I was born in 1949 and, although I spoke only Italian until I was five, English became my first language.

I suppose early experiences have profound effects. Like my father, I was sent to boarding school at the age of eight, a decent Catholic preparatory school in Worcestershire. Although I have happy memories, I can also remember how frequently I was told that 'We won the war'. This was often accompanied by a dig in the head and, truth to tell, never made me feel very English. The differences in culture were never more apparent than on visiting days, when my father was apt to kiss me. Whereas a kiss from a mother was just about tolerated, a kiss from one's father was definitely suspect, if not damn foreign.

An English public school followed, but although by this time memories of the war and its prejudices had become more remote, an Italian surname was no great help. Still, after so many years imbued with England and things English, a great deal rubbed off. In many ways this English influence is still with me, but there remains a feeling of not quite belonging. As I got older, a sense of being Italian grew in me, not replacing my early cultural adaptations, but rather in addition to them. Throughout my schooldays a holiday in Italy, or more specifically Gallinaro, was a yearly or sometimes twice yearly event. The house in Gallinaro that my father had inherited became a home from home. Here I met cousins and the children of my parents' friends, with whom I made lifelong friendships. Each visit to Italy allowed me to compare the patterns of their lives with my own, to contrast growing up in Italy with growing up in England. In my early teens, life in Italy seemed infinitely more attractive than in an English boarding school.

My parents moved from Salisbury to Dublin in 1962, while I continued boarding in England. During his years in Dublin my father was increasingly pulled towards returning to Italy. I had completed my first year at Trinity College Dublin when in 1969 my parents went back to Italy, where they remained until my father's death. It was then that perhaps I came closest to making the move to Italy myself, but an Irish wife and the lure of Ireland prevailed. Now my children can, and do, compare life in the Wicklow hills with their Italian cousins and friends.

We go to Italy every year and I hope that my children have come to love the people and places as I have. I have grown up with my friends and relations in Gallinaro, watched their careers begin and flourish, and now watch as their children grow. They have given me love and companionship over the years, as well as an understanding of how life in Italy is lived. This book is a result of the curious perspective of part belonging and part alienation with which the accidents of my personal history have left me.

# I

## *Picnics in the Snow*

My valley is a monochrome,
it knows no half-measures.
Its people are always on fire
with either love, or hate:
it takes only a drop to make them boil over.
You can't trifle with these people –
just as you can't make light of their wines.

My valley has men like pirates,
who leave, only to return
laden with booty,
to give it villas and gardens
like offerings to a spoiled lover.

My valley has women soft and gentle,
who never forget,
who live in interminable mourning.

It has boys who act like men
and treat their mothers like wives.

From *Cavallo di miniera*, by Gerardo Vacana

The valley that I also call mine, the Comino Valley, is the shape of a lozenge aligned east–west with two easy entrances, one to the west, and one to the south. It lies some eighty miles to the south-east of Rome, forming a near-equilateral triangle with Naples. Its sides are the Apennines, snow-capped for half the year, and through it flows the river Melfa, which eventually irrigates the plains of Roccasecca. Eleven towns hug the valley sides, circling the town of Gallinaro, which saddles a hill almost in the centre.

Of the twelve towns, Atina has the longest recorded history. One of the five legendary cities of Saturn, it pre-dates Rome by several centuries. It owes its historical power to its position, dominating the southern entrance to the valley which leads to the Cassino plains. As mountain valleys go, the Comino Valley is large and fertile, supporting some 25,000 inhabitants. This fertility and its defensibility have led to a long list of invaders over the years: Greeks, Samnites, Romans, Saracens, Normans, Lombards, French, Spanish, Austrians, Germans and Popes have all stayed and left their mark.

It was to this valley that my family came in the fourteenth century, to the hamlet of San Nazario in the *comune* of Casalattico. The land at San Nazario is good, sloping gently from the road to Casalattico down to the river Melfa. It was purchased from the Abbey of Montecassino in 1346 by Pasquale Fusco – the deed of sale still forms part of the incunabula of the abbey's library.

At that time the land included valley fields on both sides of the Melfa (which separates the *comune* of Casalattico from Casalvieri), the small mountain of Monte Cicuto, now in the *comune* of Atina, and the forest along the top of the Silara range which separates the Comino Valley from the plains of Cassino. Until the 1930s the farm produced corn, olives and grapes; the hillside slopes of Monte Cicuto supplied the olives that were pressed in the *frantoio* in the cellar.

The house is a large one, built upon a convent that was part of the original sale, which in turn was built upon a pre-Roman Samnite temple. By the end of the last century it was already divided into two, a result of the Italian dislike of primogeniture and a predilection for partitioning land and buildings between all the offspring equally. My great-great-grandfather, the last man to own the house intact, had three sons; one became a priest and was later to work in the Ministry of Education in the last years of the Kingdom of Naples; the other two remained in the valley to divide the house and land between them. They both had seven children, who grew up in either half of the house. The partitioning of land and house has continued. The land was divided with every generation, not into useful parcels, but by splitting each field into strips. I have inherited fifteen of these strips, totalling about 3.5 hectares; the largest strip is about half a hectare, but long and very thin. Since no strip is of any use by itself, and the chances of getting forty or so cousins together to sort it out are nil, these pieces of land are valueless and have been abandoned. Until I made them over some years ago to an uncle, I was also the possessor of a quarter of a barn, one eighth of a bedroom and one sixteenth of a kitchen.

Thankfully my father's uncle, Don Ferdinando, the arch-priest of Gallinaro, left his house there to my father and it has since come to me. From the terrace of this house I can see Monte Cicuto and La Silara, so the ancestral holdings are still in view, if nothing else.

My mother told me that as a child, growing up in Casa-lattico, she had a mental picture of the Creation. At the end of six days' labour creating the earth, God found he had nothing but rocks left over, and, throwing these away, he unwittingly created the Comino Valley. Even by Italian standards, it is high – the valley floor is more than 300 metres above sea-level and four of its towns stand at more than 600 metres. So much of Italy is mountainous, apart from the Po valley plain, which forms a triangle stretching from Turin in the west to Trieste and Rimini in the east, the rest of the peninsula is mountain, and the average width of the coastal plain is only 10 kilometres.

Topography has had its effects on the Comino Valley. Because the only two easy exits are to the west towards Rome and to the south towards Naples, the valley has always been under the influence of one or the other. Trading patterns, too, have developed along the path of least resistance westwards to Sora and Rome. Until ten years ago the road from Atina south to Cassino was a series of hairpin bends winding down from Atina, up to Belmonte, and down again to Cassino – by car a tortuous journey of about an hour. The road to Sora took about twenty-five minutes, so produce for the market was sent there instead. Contact beyond the valley has always tended to stretch westwards: Rome drew the valley's inhabitants with its jobs, hospitals and university, even though the valley had been for centuries a part of the Kingdom of Naples. Even our local dialect is closer to Roman than to Neapolitan.

All this is changing because of a new road. The *superstrada* from Atina runs south to Cassino, through a tunnel and then on stilts, in a gradual descent to the plains, so now the trip takes a little under fifteen minutes. Increasingly, produce is going to Cassino, as are the young people since the opening of the university there.

From early Roman times roads have been an important feature of the national psyche. They represent trade, progress and technological prowess. Because Italy is so mountainous, road-building requires great skill and Italian road-builders are justifiably respected for their expertise around the world. Italy spends a lot of money on roads – for the most part this is a commercial investment, allowing goods to be moved from remote areas to the market centres. It is also a part of the grander scheme of things, part of the homogenizing of all the remote pockets into a unified state. Since our valley typifies a remote region, at least topographically, we have seen at first hand the results of this strategy.

Responsibility for road-building is devolved to the four tiers of government: the national government is concerned with the building of *autostrade* and *superstrade* linking national centres; regional government builds the roads that link lesser regional centres; provincial government looks after county roads; and local government is concerned that all houses within the *comune* have access to the town's facilities. By the nature of the landscape these roads are expensive and vast sums of money are set aside for their construction. This money is distributed to the various authorities, so there is ample scope for corruption at each and every level.

Since my only viewpoint is provincial, the examples I furnish are local. However, a quick scan of the national press confirms that the local experience is universal. At my southern end of the province of Frosinone there are three centres of commerce that are important to the valley – Cassino to the south, Sora and Frosinone town to the west. For as long as anyone can remember the road from Sora to Frosinone has been horrendous. Narrow, hilly and winding, almost constantly choked with light and heavy goods vehicles, it was a perfectly formed bottle-neck. A road linking the two towns was proposed before the war, plans were laid, money set aside. By the 1980s work had begun. The section nearest to Sora was completed fairly quickly and then suddenly all activity came to a standstill.

The new road stopped where it was to span the old on a viaduct. Exactly where the viaduct was to be, the reinforced concrete skeleton of a four-storey building materialized. Years passed. It seemed that this building, obviously built without planning permission, could not be demolished perfunctorily: a long legal process had to be undergone to establish its illegality and thence to obtain an order for its destruction. The viaduct was built, the road moved on inexorably, but at a snail's pace, towards Frosinone. By 1990 another section had opened, the road a magnificent example of Italian engineering. The final section, which connects with the ring road around Frosinone, is still to be completed.

And it is at this point that, like most things in Italy, everything becomes unclear. Conspiracy theories abound and rumours are rife. You can choose which explanation to believe. Sora politicians were fighting a rearguard action, and had been for years, to stop the road. They feared a huge loss of trade if access to Frosinone became easier. On the surface a more plausible explanation was that funds had simply run out, the line followed by the local press. Another theory said, yes, funds had run out, or more precisely had been run away with. Another, which also seems likely, has it that when a road is finished and is handed over to ANAS – the national road authority – ANAS becomes responsible for its maintenance and upkeep. It appears that ANAS believes the standard to be under par and will not accept responsibility. Take your pick – all or none may be true. The fact is that the Comino

Valley area is full of road projects initiated but never finished. Even the road to Cassino from Atina stops short of its intended finishing-point, and does not currently allow access to the motorway without having to pass through Cassino itself.

The local roads have been much more of a success. In my lifetime a new road has opened up a huge hinterland of natural beauty. On the north side of the valley the town of San Donato is now the starting-point for a road which winds high up into the Apennines, over the pass of Forca d'Acero and into the Abruzzi National Park. This is a vast, unspoiled area, traditionally the preserve of shepherds, and although close geographically, was until recently as remote as Sicily. There had always been contact, of course, but only for those who had no objection to a ten-hour journey on foot, leading a mule. I know people who did the trip, trading the valley's wine for the mountain cheeses, but the contacts were sporadic and seasonal.

The effect of this road has been dramatic. Since it is now possible to drive from Cassino to San Donato in about thirty minutes, the Abruzzi National Park is a two-hour journey from Rome or Naples. In the winter the once serene, silent mountain valleys are now host to thousands of Italians on skis. Where once a few lone cross-country skiers ventured, there are bars, deck-chairs for hire, mountain rangers to supervise, police, parking problems and all that goes with an influx of humanity to a place where until recently nature was undisturbed.

The National Park was established to preserve the flora and fauna of the Apennines: here the last of Italy's brown bears, the Marsican bear, still roam free. Two packs of grey wolves live here; Apennine chamois, porcupines, martens and golden eagles are some of the wildlife that, despite the encroachment of man, survives and flourishes within the confines of the park. It is a huge reserve, straddling the boundaries of three of Italy's regions: Lazio, Molise and Abruzzo. Some of the most beautiful villages of the Abruzzi lie within the park, surrounded by heavily wooded peaks whose summits are up to 2,400 metres high.

Pescasseroli, the capital of the park, is the centre for the downhill skiers. It has a cable-car to the summit of Monte Vitelle, some 2,000 metres high, and 25 kilometres of piste. It's an enchanting village, whose older male inhabitants still carry a staff and wear the black beret and cape typical of the Abruzzi. In contrast the weekend fashion parade of Romans and Neapolitans sporting their latest ski-wear is a wonder to behold. I used to find their sartorial splendour intimidating, until I understood that in many cases the dressing-up was as close to skiing as many of them ever got. Mothers and fathers fuss and coddle small versions of their tailored selves, encouraging and cajoling – 'E sù, Marco' – until Marco finally stands upright on his tiny Rossignols. Fretting Italian mothers are torn between two conventional truths: mountain air is good for you, and children shouldn't get cold. You can see lots of tiny, red-faced Italians sweltering in portable saunas called ski-suits, while their mothers refuse to let them undo so much as a zip.

The *fondisti*, or cross-country skiers, are a hardier breed. Cross-country skiing has become a huge growth industry. Ten years ago it was a crank pastime, something Finns did in the winter. It was accepted wisdom that unless you were capable of running a two-and-a-half-hour marathon, *fondismo* was not for you. This was an image fostered by television coverage of cross-country skiing as an event at the Olympics, with lanky Scandiwegians covering 80-kilometre courses on their skis. This is not a sight readily found among the masses on a weekend in the Abruzzi mountains. Perhaps 95 per cent of those who engage in this sport neither physically resemble these champions, nor aspire to their technique of skiing. They are young and old, fat and thin – the entire gamut of human form is there, not so much for exercise as for fun.

At the pass of Forca d'Acero there is a beech-lined forestry road which slopes gently downhill to a huge natural amphi-theatre called La Macchiarvana. This is where most of the cross-country skiers gather, where the road joins the open plain. If you're feeling adventurous, from here you can set out for the wilderness, with a backpack and food. Or for the less gung-ho, like my family, we start out towing a small sled filled with wine and beer, a small charcoal grill, sausages and cured ham, *scamorza*, a local cheese that toasts to perfection, fresh crusty bread from San Donato, and perhaps a pork chop or two. We always try to get our skiing in before lunch; after a lunch with ice-cold beer and wine – we bury it in the snow – it's hard to start trekking again, especially in warm sun. On windless days it can get remarkably hot, a condition that can only be cured by more beer. Lying in the sun against one of the beeches that skirt the Macchiarvana plain, cold beer in hand, looking over the vast expanse of white, the snow-capped peaks starkly silhouetted against the dark, deep blue sky, is one of life's great pleasures.

Over the years we became very attached to these picnics in the snow. As the winters went by, friends from my village of Gallinaro started skiing and at weekends groups of up to twenty of us would set off for the mountains. I remember one occasion when I described our picnics to some friends. They thought it sounded like fun and decided to join us there. By that strange serendipity that allows Italians to meet one another when neither the time nor the place has been decided, we met up with our friends who had gathered in a little valley deep in La Macchiarvana surrounded by beech trees, miles from anywhere. We had arrived on skis, towing our sledge of victuals and pushing our baby daughter in her buggy, on which I had fitted tiny skis.

As I unpacked our picnic, I began to notice what the others had brought. A three-kilo bag of charcoal, a large, not-so-portable grill and oven combined, fifteen beef steaks, eight

9

large brown trout, a two-kilo loaf of bread, a ten-egg onion omelette, a kilo of liver sausages, seven litres of wine, four bottles of mineral water, beer, a large mixed salad in a plastic bag, a bottle of olive oil, a bottle of vinegar, a box of salt, Tabasco and a large fruit flan. Oh, yes, and a tin of corned beef. There were six of them. It was hard to make half a kilo of sausages look exciting as I unpacked beneath their watchful and slightly pitying gaze.

We built a large fire on the snow from the dead branches that were all around us; without it we would have spent the day with cold feet and wet socks. As the day passed the fire burned a deeper and deeper hole in the snow, until by evening it was a good three feet below the surface. It also became clear that skiing had assumed a distinctly lower priority than eating. The fire and the food were the principal sources of activity and conversation. The only skiing that took place was collecting wood for the fire.

The steaks were cooked on the fire embers, and eaten between slices of *pagnotta*, the large two-kilo loaf that is the Italian staple. The trout were wrapped in foil and suspended on green branches over the fire, the omelette was divided, the sausages and cheeses devoured with beer and wine. The flan was followed by a thermos of good coffee. All this under a dark blue sky with the sun blazing against the brilliance of the snow. We didn't leave until nearly five, as the gathering darkness brought the cool night air.

It was a special day for all of us. Italians love an excuse for a meal and a new location for eating is an exciting discovery. Since this meal on the snow, we have had many others, even one by the light of the full moon. The road to the Abruzzi makes one last hair-pin turn before leaving the upper edges of our valley for the pass of Forca d'Acero. The view from here is spectacular, since nearly all the valley can be seen laid out below like a scenic model railway. About twenty of us had our midnight picnic in the snow here, the lights of the towns and hamlets below us twinkling in the crispest of clear nights.

My first memory of Italian picnics is going with my uncle for a mountain picnic on the August bank holiday when I was eight. Until then, picnics had been sandwiches in a field beside a road, or sandwiches in the New Forest or sand-filled sandwiches on cloudy English beaches. I was unprepared for the Italian version. Three car-loads of family and impedimenta set off for Canneto, a sanctuary high above the town of Settefrati where the Melfa begins its course. In those days the road was what the Italians called a 'white road', which is to say its surface was non-existent. It was absurdly twisting and narrow and had no crash barriers to prevent a car from sliding off the edge into oblivion. The road arrives at the sanctuary and opens out into what was once a lake – a flat expanse of small white rocks – over which my uncle insisted on driving, cursing all the way. Uncle Alberigo had a great line in curses; he adapted litanies learnt in his youth into a list of saints who could go fuck themselves. He started with

Adriano and continued alphabetically, systematically cursing each in turn. Sudden jolts, or ominous sounding bangs from the underside of the heavily laden Fiat 1500, found the Madonna joining the saints in this list of invective.

At the far end of the old lake bed an even worse road starts to climb, roughly following the waterfalls of the upper reaches of the Melfa. Up here we drove until my Aunt Gerardella persuaded Uncle to stop. Some 20 metres below the car was the mountain stream. Across the stream, there was a small flat area of grass at the top of a waterfall, a natural terrace with a view down the valley to the Sanctuary of the Madonna. We began to unpack the picnic: not as I had suspected some sandwiches, but tables, chairs and white linen table-cloths, gas cookers and cylinders, pots and pans and food, lots of food. The men unloaded the cars, set up the tables and chairs and brought the water from the stream for boiling the pasta. The women cooked. As far as I could make out the purpose was not only to eat well, but to ensure that whatever standards of cuisine and comfort were set at home could be maintained even at the top of a mountain. This was a three-course picnic. Pasta to start, then a meat dish, and finally a dessert. As with most Italian meals on special occasions, we were eating for a good two hours. Even a natural fridge is available – all wines, beer, watermelons and fruit go into the freezing waters of the stream. We've been back to this place many times since, but there is one thing that has always been left undone – a swim in the icy waters of the mountain brook.

Mountain culture is deeply ingrained in my valley. We go to the high places for recreation, to collect wild strawberries, to gather mushrooms and plants for salads – and we go for our health. As a boy my father's brother had asthma; the cure then was a prolonged stay in the little town of Terelle. This is the highest village in Frosinone, standing at about 1,000 metres above sea level. Although the *comuni* of Terelle and Casa-

lattico border one another, by road the journey was long –
from Casalattico to Atina, the winding road to Cassino, and
then doubling back up the hairpin bends to Terelle, a car
journey of some two hours. From Atina a new mountain
road now gets you directly to this little town with its stunning
chestnut groves in about twenty minutes. These chestnut
groves are the last remaining in our province; they surround
the lower reaches of the town and during the heat of the
summer there is cool mountain air and shade.

The area of mountain forest along the ridge of La Silara
above Casalattico, a part of the family patrimony that has
come to me, was for many years something I looked at
proprietorially from the valley floor. Not relishing the prospect of a three-hour uphill climb along overgrown mule
tracks, I contented myself with long-range visual inspections
of my forest. Well, to be exact, I inspected what I thought
was my bit. My grandmother Luisa, who left me this piece of
forest, was never too clear as to its exact location. When
pressed by me, she would point vaguely at the ridge and say,
'It's up there.' I am still not entirely sure which bit is mine,
but since there is not much I can do with it anyway, it's not
really a problem.

Now I can drive to within a kilometre of where I think it
is, and do so regularly. A terrifying, unsurfaced road runs up
the side of Monte Prato from Atina, and continues along the
ridge of La Silara. The views are sensational. To the north,
spread out below, lies the Comino Valley, visible practically
in its entirety; to the south the Monte Cairo Valley stretching
down to the Cassino plains. You can see Belmonte, Terelle,
the town of Cassino and the abbey of Montecassino, with the
horizon disappearing into the haze. Along this ridge are the
scars of war. There are bomb craters and fox-holes, part of
what was once the Cassino line. Almost at the summit of La
Silara is a small area of pasture, and five Samnite wells. They
are called wells, but are in fact huge cisterns that collect the

winter rain in this natural basin. Even in the driest of summers there is always cool water deep down the cisterns. Places like the five wells have remained unspoiled because of their inaccessibility, but expansion into previously remote areas will certainly continue, as increasingly mobile and affluent Italians demand more space. Currently the density of the Italian population is on a par with India.

When I was twelve, my cousin Gigino took me to the top of Monte Cicuto, a small hill to the west of Atina where the family olive groves are. We drove to La Macchia, a hamlet of Casalattico, and then walked from there to the summit. It was my first recollection of seeing so much of the valley at one go. Immediately below was the bridge over the river Melfa, connecting Atina to the rest of valley. I could see the garage, the hotel and the few scattered houses that made up Ponte Melfa. Today, from the same vantage point, now reached by tarmac road, Ponte Melfa looks like a miniature Hong Kong. Dense, high-rise buildings line the banks of the river, housing developments stretch up the surrounding hillsides, an industrial estate lies downstream, the skeleton of a huge hospital is taking shape, a hippodrome and go-kart track invade more of what was once green. So meteoric has the growth of Ponte Melfa been, fuelled in part by the new road to Cassino, that moves are afoot to establish it as a *comune* in its own right. The majority of the citizens of Atina now live there rather than in the old town on the hill.

Monte Cicuto is still largely unspoiled. Amid the olive groves there is a small cottage, which now belongs to my uncle. Originally it was a *casa colonica*, a house for the farmworkers, who were given the house under the old system of land use, whereby the landlord let the land in return for half the produce – a system unchanged for centuries. Gradually I have discovered its drawbacks as an absentee landlord: my strip of olive grove on Monte Cicuto has produced, over twenty or so years, 1.5 litres of oil as my share.

CASA COLONICA

It was in this cottage on Monte Cicuto that my father and his cousin Dino hid from the Germans from October 1943 to February 1944, while the Gustav line at Cassino was established. When Italy broke with the Axis powers on 25 July 1943, my father, still officially in the Italian army, needed to keep his head down. On that July day, which also happened to be the day his grandfather died, he took off his uniform and walked home from Rome, avoiding roads and keeping to the hills. When Monte Cicuto itself was declared a war zone by the Germans, the family moved *en masse* to the hills above Arpino, burying as much of their belongings as they could in a cave. They stayed here until the end of May 1944, when the Allies finally took Cassino and liberated the valley. For them, at least, the war had ended.

Despite massive post-war emigration, the Italian economic boom has continued unabated here, so much so that the valley, once a source of manual labour for Rome, and desperately poor, is now one of the most expensive parts of Italy in which to buy land. It must be said that the price of land is so high not only because of the economic upturn in the valley's fortunes, but also because of capital returning from abroad. The diaspora that so impoverished the valley in the late 1940s and 1950s is now being reversed. The *émigrés* who have made their fortunes have been coming home, bringing their capital with them. Many of those who left were landless, and the dream of returning always carried with it the need for land on which to plant a vineyard and on which to build a house. Their determination to buy land at virtually any cost pushed prices on occasion up to £8,000 or £9,000 an acre, at least four times as much as similar land in Tuscany.

A trip around the valley towns in August shows clearly who emigrated to where. In Casalattico and its hamlets the roads are filled with cars with IRL stickers, or in the case of Mortale, GB stickers. Mortale, a small hamlet, has recently had its name changed officially to Monforte. This is to honour its most illustrious son, Lord Charles Forte, who came from here. Recently he has been spending more and more time in Casalattico, where he is held in high regard, especially since he paid for the floodlighting of the football pitch. In Atina you find GB, in Gallinaro F and B. Germany, Venezuela, America, Argentina and Australia became home to many from the valley. As Italy's fortunes improved – it is now ranked sixth among the world's economies – so homesickness and perceived opportunities have brought many of the emigrants home.

For some of those who remained, the returning emigrant has been a lucrative source of income. 'A chicken ripe for plucking' is a phrase often used to describe the emigrants, and plucked of their feathers many of them have been – a few emigrating a second time, perhaps to rebuild their fortunes.

They pay too much for the land they buy, too much to the builders of their houses, too much to builders' suppliers and often not enough to people in public office who could help them through the tangled web of regulation and red tape that is Italian bureaucracy.

This particular minefield, the Italian bureaucracy, can be an impenetrable labyrinth to the uninitiated. It has driven a couple I met, recently returned from Scotland, right back to the safe, honest, Presbyterian haven of Aberdeen. The closest a casual visitor or tourist is likely to come to this bureaucracy is in an Italian bank. To change bank notes – in any other country an operation of blinding simplicity – involves a minimum of two queues, and probably the need to produce a passport and forms signed in triplicate. Any Italian bank will be full of men in shirt-sleeves behind the counter, all purposefully shuffling papers and moving from desk to desk, completely ignoring the customers. Tellers shut their doors for no apparent reason and disappear. Anything more complicated than changing money can take hours, or in some cases days. Queues in banks, by the way, are exactly the same as most Italian queues – that is, the order of precedence is not often first come, first served. Favoured customers are taken in behind the counter to do their business while lesser mortals wait at unmanned tellers' windows. Town halls and post offices are identical in their view of customer service.

In the 1970s my parents opened an antique shop in Sora, specializing in English furniture. Having rented the ground floor of a new building, they needed only a fire certificate to open. My mother asked her friends how to proceed. 'Easy,' they said. 'Go to Frosinone Head Office, and give the fire chief a million lire [about £500], and he'll give you the certificate.' My mother, who had spent many years in England and admired the English way of doing things, was horrified. The idea of paying a bribe to get something that was hers by right appalled her. She refused, and waited six months in vain for a certificate allowing the shop to open. Eventually she did as her friends suggested, paid the chief and got the certificate, having lost six months' trade.

# 2

# *Wine and the Baby Jesus*

August is busy in Gallinaro, it's the month when all the emigrants return, and it's the month of the *festa* of San Gerardo, patron saint of the village. Small villages like mine rarely have much claim to fame, but the English pilgrim, Gerard, who became its patron saint, left a legacy of at least regional fame for his adopted village.

Conversion to Christianity began in earnest in the British Isles in the early seventh century. Pope Gregory the Great had sent Saint Augustine to begin the task. At the same time, in 628, Cyrus, King of the Persians, was compelled by the Byzantine emperor Heraclius to return the True Cross, which he, Cyrus, had stolen in 627 when he had sacked Jerusalem. Heraclius let it be known throughout Christendom that the cross would be returned to Jerusalem the following year, 629. From all over the Christian world pilgrims set out to arrive in Jerusalem by that date, among them four English converts, whose names have come to us as Gerard, Bernard, Arduine and Folco. They were in Jerusalem when Heraclius himself reinstalled the True Cross in the Basilica of Jerusalem.

After a short stay in the Holy Land, the four set off for home in 630, travelling through Italy from Bari to Monte Gargano, where the Archangel Michael had appeared to Pope Gelasius I. There they spent nine years fasting, praying and teaching. Eventually resuming their journey to Rome, they stopped for a while in the Comino Valley, where all four fell prey to fever. Gerard, now fifty-two years old, succumbed and died in Gallinaro in April 639. His three companions moved on towards Rome, but Bernard died after a little way in Rocca d'Arce, Folco in Santo Padre, and Arduine in Ceprano – they are all now patron saint of the town in which they died.

In 655 a dying traveller spent the night in Gallinaro beside St Gerard's tomb. He had a vision of the saint, who told him that the people of Gallinaro were poor and ungrateful. On awakening he found himself in full health. The miracles had begun. Local legend has it that many of Gerard's family were present for his canonization and took the name Gerard henceforth as their surname. In 1355 a knight called Dominic de Gerardis arrived in Gallinaro to pay homage to Saint Gerard. In 1376 two knights, Peter and Andrew de Gerardis, also came to Gallinaro. Sir Peter, a priest, gave money and land to the parish, while Sir Andrew founded a public hospital for the poor, which, although long gone, is remembered in the name of the road to Ponte Melfa, still called Via Ospedale.

Perhaps the most illustrious of the Gerard family arrived in 1608. John Gerard of the Society of Jesus, founder of the English College in Douai, one of the only men ever to escape from the Tower of London, came to honour his ancestor. He brought a gift of a silver monstrance, made in the shape of an arm and inscribed *'Anglicana Gerardorum familia suasu, atque opera Patris Johannes de Gerardi e societate Jesu dono mittit anno salutis MDCVIII'*, roughly translated as 'Through the aegis of Father John Gerard SJ the English family of Gerard sends this gift, this year of grace 1608'. This monstrance still leads the processions that are held in honour of the saint.

My old friend Domenico Celestino disputes many of the legends concerning our patron saint.

'Fifteenth-century fantasy,' he said. 'Gerardo couldn't have come here in the seventh century, Gallinaro didn't exist till the tenth. The hagiographers liked to drag as many mystical and magical elements as they could into the lives of the saints, hence all that guff about the True Cross and the Emperor Heraclius. All made up to titillate and enthral the faithful – those hagiographies were the fifteenth-century equivalent of romantic thrillers.'

I reminded him that he had subtitled his book on the history of Gallinaro '*Twenty Centuries on a Hill*'. By my reckoning that put the founding of Gallinaro at around the year dot.

He was not to be dissuaded. He had found in the episcopal records in Sora documents relating to the canonization of our saint. According to these, Gerardo died in Gallinaro in 1102, and was canonized by Bishop Roffredo of Sora in 1127. These documents run counter to the oral tradition which has always maintained that he was English; the Sora records on three occasions say he was from Alvernia in France. It is possible that he may have been of Norman descent and origin, and, although French, he may have come from Norman-occupied England. This, coupled with the well-documented evidence of the fourteenth-century visit of the two English knights, and the seventeenth-century visit of John Gerard, probably makes this version essentially correct.

Since the miracle of the traveller, pilgrims have come from all over the region to the Sanctuary of San Gerardo. The town of Scanno, high up in the Abruzzi mountains, still sends the largest group, normally around one hundred, who come on his feast day to reclaim the saint that they feel is rightfully theirs. It was in Scanno that the saint had spent his nine years of missionary work; his only connection with Gallinaro was that its unwholesome air had caused his death.

Nowadays the new road through Forca d'Acero means the Scannese can come by bus, but I can remember seeing their torchlit procession coming down the mountains, a journey which took two days on foot. Today they walk only from the bottom of the hill up to the town, some 3 kilometres. It is still an event steeped in ritual. The Scannese arrive in their traditional costumes, the women with beautifully embroidered dresses and head-scarves, the men in black capes. All of them carry a staff for the procession and sing as they walk. Men and women alternate verses in a hymn of praise to San Gerardo. They spend the night in the church, ready for the *festa* the next morning.

Despite this continuing devotion, it has been many years since the good saint has performed a miracle. Why there should be this lapse after so many years of performing, I don't know. However, miracles have not stopped in Gallinaro. While San Gerardo has been on the wane, another site of miracles has been established in a woodland clearing in the valley just below my house.

Some twenty years ago a Gallinaro woman was working her land when she had a vision of the Virgin Mary cradling the baby Jesus in her arms. She was inspired to build a small chapel on the site of her vision, nestled between olive trees, with a backdrop of Gallinaro spread out along the ridge and the high Apennines behind. This tiny chapel, known as the 'Bambin' Gesù di Gallinaro' or the 'Baby Jesus of Gallinaro', surrounded by wood violets and anemones, now attracts pilgrims on a daily basis. In the last few years it has mushroomed into a phenomenon that is impossible to ignore. On Sundays in summer an average of 150 coaches and 400 to 500 cars arrive, turning this tiny village into a sort of embryonic Lourdes.

So large is this influx that the town council has had to make changes to accommodate it. The official market day was changed from Friday to Sunday, so that now townspeople can legally sell their produce to the pilgrims who have to walk the last 2 kilometres to the chapel, passing an increasingly large assortment of restaurants, bars and stalls. Large placards on the roadsides modestly inform the visitors that they are entering the confines of the New Jerusalem. The feeling is mixed in the town as to the merits of having miracles; some five families benefit from the trade that so many people bring, but the rest of us have to put up with the rubbish and the choked access roads.

To accommodate so many coaches in this mountain village, another road had to be built, almost parallel to the old, making each one-way only. Where once the view from our *terrazza* was of unspoilt valley, now the new road passes directly behind the garden wall, giving us a view of the coaches' roofs as they pass. And it seems that the development won't stop there. The small valley we look out upon will almost certainly have yet another new road cut through it from the west, allowing direct access to the Chapel of the Baby Jesus from Sora and Rome, by-passing Gallinaro completely. There is even a scheme to build a large pilgrims' complex in this same valley to accommodate pilgrims who want to spend more than a day at the shrine. Recently I have begun to notice road signs as much as 50 kilometres away pointing the way to the chapel.

Italy, like most countries in Europe, is becoming increasingly secular. The phenomenon of the Baby Jesus of Gallinaro is probably the last gasp of an old order. The pilgrims who flock to the shrine are mostly old, and the majority are from the south of Italy. The letters on Italian number-plates denote the province in which the car owner is resident, and a cursory glance shows almost none of the cars come from north of Rome. It may be a gross generalization, but the industrial north is less inclined to believe in miracles than the agricultural south, and the young are similarly inclined to disbelief.

A typical example of what sort of miracle to expect took place in July 1993. Nearly a thousand pilgrims witnessed the sun split in two. One half continued its normal course, the other went backwards. Curiously, although this event was reported in the regional press, the phenomenon was not visible from my terrace, where the sun kept to its usual itinerary. As far as I know, no observatory in the world noticed this odd happening either.

Creeping secularization has also had an effect on the *festa* of San Gerardo, as the religious aspects of the festival have increasingly been overshadowed by fun. People from other villages have long come, not for the mass and the processions, but for the dancing, the band and the fair that makes up the rest of the three-day *festa*. In 1991 the town council decided to append a five-day secular festival to the three-day 'religious' one. It was called the 'Festa per quelli che tornano'. 'Those who return' refers to the town's emigrants scattered around the globe.

The valley has seen times of abundance and times of poverty. When in 1944 General Kesselring was driven from the valley by the Allies, a new era dawned. Within five years economic desperation forced nearly half of the inhabitants to leave. The town of Casalattico now has a population of just over 600; over 2,000 of its inhabitants are in Dublin. The migration of the landless had its effects upon the landed as well – since no one was left to work on the farms, many of the farmers gave up the struggle and emigrated as well. Every member of my family, except for two spinster aunts, left, leaving the farm for ever, after 600 years of occupancy.

For eleven months of the year Gallinaro has a population of around 600; in August when the emigrants return it becomes thousands. They have for years been a mainstay of the local economy, not just because of what they spend in the month of August, but also because of money they have sent to dependent relatives over the years and the money they spend rebuilding their family houses, or constructing new ones. A festival to encourage their continuing return is clearly a worthwhile investment.

It began uncontroversially enough on 4 August with a painting competition: the contestants were required to paint any aspect of the town within the time limit of eight in the morning to five in the evening. Throughout the day artists, including my wife, worked all around the town, their picnic lunch supplied and delivered *in situ* courtesy of the town council. During the afternoon the heats of the ping-pong competition took place noisily in the piazza. By six o'clock the paintings were framed and hung, some twenty of them, on the wall of the old *palazzo* that flanks one side of the piazza. While we were viewing the exhibition Alberto, the mayor, approached me.

'Are you still in the wine business?' he asked.

I told him I was.

'Good,' he said, 'I need you on the tasting panel for the wine competition.'

Now this represented something of a poisoned chalice in more ways than one. Gallinaro wine-makers pride themselves on their cabernet sauvignon, each producer fiercely proud of his own wine and positively disdainful of anyone else's. I can count about twenty producers between friends and relations, so here was an opportunity to offend virtually everyone I know. However he insisted, and I accepted.

One of my oldest friends in Gallinaro is Nicola Celestino. He offered to show me to the new town hall where the tasting was to take place. We were at the door when he said to me: 'You'll know my wine, it's a white, but with a hint of rosé; I'll say no more.'

Every year Nicola has given me a 25-litre demijohn of his wine; now was clearly the moment for the favour to be repaid.

Inside the town hall I found a large table with nine panel members already seated around it, but no wine as yet in sight. The jury was made up of two wine merchants from nearby towns, the president of the wine co-operative Cesanese del Piglio, his son and the export manager, an emigrant to France back for the holidays, a small, neat man who looked exactly like Suchet's Poirot, two wine lovers from adjacent towns, and me. The mayor arrived, introduced us to each other and explained how the tasting was to work. The producers had entered two bottles of each wine presented, one with their name and address inside a closed envelope sealed to the bottle with wax, the other with only a number. We were to see only the numbered bottles. In this way no one could know whose wine was being tasted and the integrity of the competition would be assured.

It was now half past six. The mayor explained that there were eighty-seven wines to be tasted, and that the presentation was due to be made on the stage in the piazza at nine o'clock. It would be a rushed job, but if we started now, it might just be possible. One of the wine merchants suggested that we should have a chairman and so a long discussion took place to decide who that might be. Eventually it was decided that the small, neat man, the owner of a fine walled vineyard in Sant' Elia Fiume Rapido where he produces and bottles an excellent merlot, should have the honour. Another ten minutes was then lost while glasses, paper for notes, pens and a bottle opener were sought and found. Ten to seven, and nineteen white wines were placed on the table.

We decided that in order not to influence each other unduly we would score all nineteen wines and only then read out our marks for each, which would be totalled and divided by ten. About half-way through the bottles a rosé was poured. Nicola's wine. It was delicious and I marked it high. By eight o'clock we were reading out our marks for the whites. Nicola won hands down. This was becoming embarrassing.

Our chairman suggested we should taste the top five wines again, since these were to be presented with diplomas of excellence, just in case we wanted to revise our original judgements. Nicola was still winning. Our chairman tried another tack. 'This winning wine,' he said, 'is more a rosé than a white. Perhaps it should have first prize as a rosé.'

There was some agreement with this, when Diodato, one of the wine merchants (with whom Nicola shares a house), remarked that it could look as though it had won by virtue of being the only rosé, not because it had had higher marks than any of the whites. A compromise was reached: it would win first prize as rosé and our chairman would take pains to point out at the prize-giving that it was first on merit, rather than because it was the only contestant in the category.

It was ten past eight, I had had no supper and there were sixty-eight red wines still to taste. The mayor arrived with news of the painting competition. The jury had nearly come to blows over who was to receive the first prize. It seems that my friend Nicola had phoned the mayor the previous week and had suggested an art teacher that he knew as a possible member of the jury. The mayor had accepted his recommendation and put the teacher on the jury. Now it transpired that one of the contestants, a pretty girl from Poland and a cousin of Nicola's latest girlfriend, happened to be the object of this art teacher's affections. He had helped with her composition throughout the day and was holding out for her to win first prize. The other members of the jury didn't want to even place her work, but eventually they arrived at the compromise of adding a sixth prize and awarding it to her. My wife, the mayor told me, had won third prize, and would have won first prize if she hadn't entered a water-colour. Still, third prize was 300,000 lire, in cash.

I wasn't the only member of the panel to be hungry. The others complained that they needed food to continue with this arduous task. Bread and cheese arrived; it was quarter past eight. Clearly there would be no prize-giving at nine o'clock. More discussion, more bread and cheese, more time lost. Our chairman suggested a solution. We would now make a selection of the twenty best reds, and at ten o'clock we would taste them once more on the stage in the piazza for their final placings.

And so it was that for the next hour and a half about thirty of the most unpleasant wines I have ever tasted hit my palate like liquid trip-hammers. After three of these in succession, the Frenchman announced that since his palate was accustomed to only the finest clarets, he would retire from the panel and left. Unfortunately, because of where I was sitting, the first glass of each wine now came to me, instead of to the Frenchman, ensuring that I tasted all thirty of the poisonous bottles, while my fellow panellists, having watched my reactions, were able to avoid them. Out of the forty or so wines that were drinkable, finding twenty finalists was not too hard.

Ten o'clock found us at the rear of the stage under the glare of the spotlights, tasting the final twenty once more while local poets read dialect poems and stories, emceed by a personable young man from Radio Sora. At eleven o'clock the MC announced that the results of the wine-tasting and the prize-giving would take place on Thursday, 8 August.

As the next few days passed in a flurry of music, fireworks, dancing and indigenous sports, the full weight of the responsibility I had accepted became increasingly apparent. There was no escape from talk of wine, juries and honesty. Every winemaker in the village buttonholed me at some stage, since I was the only juror who was permanently in the village.

'Did you taste my wine? Good, wasn't it?'

All attempts to explain the intricacies that had been observed to ensure anonymity were greeted with a knowing wink. Everyone was sure that the jury was voting by any criterion other than honesty.

On Thursday afternoon I went to photograph *gl'palluot*, a game of obscure origins that once involved rolling hard cheeses down a hill. Nowadays it is played with a thick wooden disk, 20 centimetres in diameter; a string is whipped round it, and the player holds one end while hurling the *palluot* along the road. The rules are simple enough: teams of four players take it in turn to throw the disk from where the last throw ended. The team with the fewest throws to complete the course wins. Less than fifty throws for the 5-kilometre course is championship class.

The course for the event starts below the main church where the road begins to slope down towards San Donato; at the foot of the hill there is a pause, at my grandfather's house, where refreshments such as wine and beer are served. When the last team finishes the downhill, the game continues back up to the church. Along the route there are drinking stops, where wine is served from a tractor and trailer to contestants and spectators alike. Most of the people whose houses line this stretch are also on the roadside, offering wine to passers-by. In the past I have been foolish enough to accept hospitality wherever it was offered on the way down, making the way back difficult. The skill in this game is twofold: throwing the *palluot* at the correct angle to negotiate bends in the road, thus gaining distance; and staying sober. Some players could barely stand when they arrived at the finish, while Michele, who was driving the tractor, was having difficulty staying on the road.

I walked along part of the route with Nino, the mayor's brother, an old friend. The idea for the wine-tasting was originally his, he told me. Nino is an avid wine-maker, and he had assembled a jury with himself as president, but had been overruled by my good friend Graziano, currently a town councillor and in charge of the festival. Nino was thoroughly disgruntled at what he perceived to be a hijacking of his idea and his chance to head a tasting panel. However, he was prepared to accept that the new panel would stand a better chance of being seen to be impartial and expressed the hope that it had been just that. I assured him that we had behaved impeccably.

On Thursday night the piazza was full. An orchestra from Emilia-Romagna were playing *liscio*, smoochy 1960s' dance music. During the break the mayor was called to the stage by the MC, the panel were invited to take their places at the rear of the stage, and the prize-giving began. Every participant received a certificate inscribed by a hired calligrapher, who now took his place on the stage, as each of the sealed bottles was opened in turn, and the names of the producers were matched to the numbered bottles. A cry of 'fix' went up as Nicola collected his certificate and trophy for the best rosé, not before it had been suitably eulogized by the panel's chairman. All the bottles were opened and distributed among the crowd, so that everyone could taste the wines and compare their own impressions with those of the jury.

We came to the last three reds, the cabernets, the ones that mattered. Third place was won by a man who sells wine commercially in large quantity. Not much argument there. Second place went to a man who has no vineyard. The hecklers were in full cry. 'He buys all his grapes! How can he win a prize when the grapes aren't from Gallinaro? He gets the grapes from Le Puglie.'

The mayor called for hush. 'And the first prize goes to Loreto Lucarelli!' Loreto is the father of Graziano, the councillor who organized the event. The implications of this decision took a while to sink in.

I made my way quickly to the back of the stage while the prizes were handed out, ready to do a runner. A hand tugged at my trousers. I looked down at one of the producers from the slopes to the west of the village.

'Excuse me, but do you know how to make wine?' The implications of this question were clearly insulting.

'Yes,' I replied, 'it's made with sugar, bull's blood and industrial alcohol.' Sometimes the best defence is offence.

The back of the stage was now cut off by a mass of people. Rafaele, a smallholder, handed me two magnums, one of red, one of white. 'Taste those,' he commanded. Both were excellent. All around me milled the orchestra, the tasting panel, the town councillors and irate producers, these last all clamouring for a taste of the winning wine and explanations as to why they hadn't won.

Nino arrived on the stage to join the mêlée. I asked how had he done. 'Not placed.' He wandered off, sulkily. No prizes and his idea hijacked.

Beside me a man confronted our chairman with a bottle of his wine. 'Taste this again. How can it not be placed?'

I watched with interest as the chief taster once again appraised the wine.

'Well?' demanded its maker.

'You fermented this in an oak barrel, didn't you?'

'No.'

'Then you used a fibreglass container.'

'No.'

'In a glass demijohn?'

'Yes.'

'Aha!' he exclaimed triumphantly. 'This is typical of wine fermented in glass. That's why it wasn't placed.'

This was delivered with such conviction that the producer left with his bottle, stupefied into submission by the erudition of the chairman.

Rafaele, the smallholder with the good wine, approached again. 'Isn't that the best wine you've tasted?' He eyed the chairman and myself like a hawk.

It certainly was the best I'd tasted, but it had not won a prize. The chairman, clearly as puzzled as I was, spoke. 'It's very good, but . . .'

We were saved any further pain: 'Damn right it's good. That's why I didn't enter it. Too good for this lot.' And off he went, beaming with pleasure at having made his point.

I slunk off home to eat, but the fall-out didn't end there. Graziano arrived at my door.

'I'm delighted that we won,' he said, 'but no one believes it wasn't fixed.'

In Italy there is a general inability to see things as uncomplicated even if they really are. An explanation of events that includes conspiracies, double-dealing and machiavellian machinations will always be preferred to one without these ingredients. Although the organizers had gone to great lengths to preserve the anonymity of each bottle, it was clear to all from the result that somehow the jury had been rigged and that the Lucarelli wine had been preferred over better wines. And what about Nicola? Hadn't he also managed to win, surely by getting at the jury? The truth, I suppose, lies somewhere between honesty and rigging. Nicola's wine would probably have won even without my votes and Loreto's win was really fair and square, but the fact remains that some attempt at jury rigging had been possible.

Nino found me in the bar the next day. He bought me a drink and looked me piercingly in the eye.

'You recognized Nicola's wine, didn't you?'

I didn't lie. 'Yes, I did.'

'I knew it! The sly shit. He can't let anything happen without trying to muddy the waters. So, not content with trying to fix the painting contest, he had a go at the wine jury too. I knew it!'

I explained that his wine was good and, anyway, since it was the only rosé, it couldn't fail to win a prize.

He remained unconvinced. 'If we want this to be the first of many wine competitions, this is the sort of thing that we have to avoid.'

And so it is. The plans are already laid for next year. Identical bottles will be issued to the contestants so that no one can describe the peculiarities of their bottle to the jury. The two-bottle system will remain, but the number on the numbered bottle will be covered, so the jury cannot see it. Only after it is tasted and voted upon will it be unmasked. But whatever refinements go into making sure justice is seen to be done, the inventiveness of the Italians will surely find a way around it.

# 3

# *Casa Nostra*

Gallinaro is long and thin. It stretches along the crest of a hill for around 2 kilometres, for much of the way only one house deep on either side of the road. At the highest point, around the church, the town spreads out into a maze of narrow cobbled alleys, wide enough for a laden donkey to pass. Below the church, there is just room for a long, thin piazza, not much wider than the road.

My house opens off the road. From the front it is a two-storey house with only four windows facing the street, all on the first floor. The street is narrow and the houses on the other side are tall, so the front of the house is mostly in shade. With the lack of windows at street level, this makes the entrance gloomy. Just inside the door there is a dark, black staircase to the first floor. At the top there is a small, formal sitting-room, with a balcony on the street side and double doors leading to the roof terrace on the other. After the gloom of the stairs, the first floor seems ablaze with light.

The *terrazza* is a big one, 8 by 5 metres, from which two thirds of the Comino Valley is visible. It is hard to describe the scale of the view. The *terrazza* looks nearly due west and on a clear day, such as after a thunderstorm, you can see Veroli, a town 37 kilometres away as the crow flies. As you look westwards, the Apennines rise on the right; on hazy days only those that encircle the valley are visible, but sometimes you can see the higher mountains behind them,

and sometimes the even higher ones beyond. The Silara range is on the left, cleft in the middle where a deep, steep-sided gorge has been cut through by the river Melfa. Before you stretches the valley, past the old Norman keep at Vicalvi and the lake at Posta Fibreno, almost as far as Sora. The valley is wide below Gallinaro, but tapers to the west, towards Vicalvi.

The light is extraordinary and ever-changing. My wife, an artist, sits for hours trying to capture the ephemeral plays of light in water-colours. The view is never the same; distant hills come in and out of sight, sometimes Alvito seeming absurdly close and at other times just visible through the haze. The pattern made on the land by terraces, olive groves and vineyards seen from a distance is like marquetry of great complexity and beauty.

Whenever I am at home in Ireland and think of the house in Gallinaro I invariably find myself mentally on the *terrazza*. When we arrive it's the first place I go to. As you lean on the railings that surround it, below is a drop of two storeys to the garden, since the house has three storeys at the back. Beyond the garden wall there is another drop to the new road; beyond that the land falls sharply away to the valley floor, nearly 215 metres below. The feeling of height on the *terrazza* is strong.

The right-hand side of the *terrazza* looks out on to the old part of the town. We probably have the most uninterrupted view of the church in the village; nowhere else can so much of it be seen at once. It is a massive, thick-walled building that was once a Norman castle. Behind it you can see the road to Forca d'Acero snaking up into the mountains, making its last turn out of the valley as it enters the pass. Since the house once belonged to my great-uncle, the archpriest, the view of the church seems curiously apt. The houses in the old part of the town cascade from the church down to the road, their roofs almost blending into a waterfall of tiles. We can just see the entrance to Bar Sinella; people take their drinks and ice-creams and sit on the wall that edges the road to look, to be seen and to chat. No one can pass through Gallinaro without passing this spot. This is where you go to find people or to be found. To the left of the *terrazza* we look down to a small public garden and not much else; the view is blocked by a huge walnut tree that drops its nuts into our garden.

At night the panorama from the *terrazza* is magnificent. The lights of the towns and the floodlights on their churches and civic buildings sparkle in the night air. In summer this visual delight is accompanied by the continuous singing of the *grilli* – crickets by night and cicadas by day. The first thing a visitor notices is the noise – not loud, but incessant. Birds and *grilli* sing their songs, agricultural machinery drones in the terraced hillsides, the people chat and shout in the

streets. Cars and motorcycles seem to have exhausts specially tuned all the better to be heard.

In August the season starts in earnest. Every town, every hamlet has a *festa* and every *festa* has music, dancing and fireworks. In August 1991 there were eighty-five civic events and *feste* in the valley. The fireworks are the single most expensive item. They are the visible and audible manifestation of the event, the best-attended part of the *festa* and the most eagerly awaited.

On a summer's night, sitting in the warm air on the *terrazza*, we can see the firework displays not just in the valley but even from Arpino and Sora. I can remember a night when we came home after a dinner, replete and full of wine. A thunderstorm was raging in the Apennines, sheet and forked lightning lit the skies and the mountains behind Alvito, creating an almost theatrical backdrop. It can't have been raining in Alvito, as the firework display was in full swing. Being one of the largest towns in the valley, it has money to spend on its fireworks and for nearly half an hour I watched as the foreground filled with bursts of blue, green and red, cascades of white fire, rockets and fire fountains, while in the background nature's own display raged. I tried, without success, to photograph it, using thirty-second exposures, but either nothing happened for thirty seconds or a lot did, so the resulting pictures were either black or over-exposed by sheet lightning.

In September thunderstorms tend to arrive in the afternoon, bang and flash for an hour or so and then go away again, leaving the air clear of dust when the sun returns. These short, sharp storms are fun to observe from the *terrazza*. The half-roof keeps you dry while you watch its arrival, normally from the south-west, then its mighty display and finally its disappearance. Being able to see so far means that you can spot a front coming from tens of miles away and watch its development as it heads for the valley. Sometimes the weather can be dramatic. On a warm evening, 16 August 1991, the sky became a violent shade of yellow, and huge hail-stones started to fall. Most were larger than golf balls; the largest one I saw – preserved in Sinella's deep-freeze – was the size of a tennis ball. They fell with terrifying speed and caused immense damage to the ripening grapes on Gallinaro's slopes. Bruised grapes do not ripen, they rot. For half an hour the hail-stones broke roof tiles, windows and three car windscreens. My car still carries the dents on the bonnet, roof and boot of this savage hail. No one was injured, but two cows died, either from a direct hit or from shock. Again, we watched this ferocity from the *terrazza,* huge lumps of ice shattering on the tiled floor, sending fragments in all directions. An hour later the streets, white for a little while, were steaming in the evening sun. It was as if the savagery of the storm had never happened; only the dented car is there to remind me that it did.

The *terrazza* is where we eat lunch *al fresco* every day – normally a cold collation, such as fresh bread, *mozzarella, prosciutto* and cold beer. Until about two o'clock there is enough shade to be comfortable, but as the sun comes round and shines straight in it is time to go. Because the *terrazza* faces west, we return to watch the sun go down. In June the sun sets perfectly in the pass at Vicalvi, low, impossibly big and very red. Any clouds in the sky are lit from below with a flame-orange glow. The dust in the air creates strange and unlikely colours – green, violet and dark reds. These sunsets are so improbable that, were they painted, they would be seen as a flight of artistic fancy. The back wall of the *terrazza* and its now rather faded fresco turn from white to pink for those few magical moments before the sun finally disappears.

Recently I was looking through old photographs, going back to the turn of the century. People that I recognize and some that I don't are posing on the *terrazza.* There is something strange about seeing people you know are no longer alive in a place that is so familiar and unchanged. It makes me feel less of an owner and more of a caretaker of the house, tending it in my lifetime to pass it on to the next generation. In the photographs the fresco looks brighter, but little else has changed. Only the vines, which had been trained up the walls from the garden to roof the *terrazza* with greenery, are gone now. There was a pleasure in standing on the *terrazza* in September and picking the luscious bunches of table grapes straight from the vine. Unfortunately vines, like everything else, have their allotted span and these venerable plants were eventually killed by a savage winter frost in 1976.

The balcony on the other side of the house is just big enough for a couple of chairs. Opening the double doors and sitting on the balcony has a twofold significance: you can see what happens in the street, and you can be seen. Anyone who passes, or indeed anyone on the facing balconies, presumes that you are ready for a chat. It is a wonderful combination – you're in your house, but still able to partake of the public life outside. Many Italians without balconies sit at their front door to obtain the same effect. Balconies figure largely in Neapolitan love songs, since young girls were not allowed out of the house at night, but could still see and be seen by admirers on the balcony. Shakespeare had it right when he put Juliet on a balcony. This is naturally where we go to watch the processions that form an integral part of the *feste*. I have become used to seeing the top of San Gerardo's head, as the saint is carried from his sanctuary down the hill up to the main church for mass and then down again. This is accompanied by a wailing tune with the refrain '*E viva San Gerardo prottetore*' – 'Long live St Gerard, our protector'. I have endless videos of these processions, of interest to no one but myself, and most of them have a sea of heads passing below the balcony, among them plenty of upturned smiling faces and accompanying waves to the video camera.

The dining-room in Italian houses is important, often purpose-built. Given their love of food and dining in company, this is not surprising. Our dining-room in Gallinaro is the largest room in the house, its windows and balcony opening on to the same wonderful view of the valley. As a young man, my father found an old cabinet-maker in Fiuggi, aged eighty and nearing retirement. He persuaded him to

take on one last commission. The resulting furniture dominates the room — a table that seats up to twelve, a sideboard and a piece for which I know no name; it looks like a sideboard but has cupboards mounted above, integral with it. These three pieces and the chairs are walnut and are heavily and intricately carved. I've always liked them and last summer was upset to find that polecats had got into the house during our absence and had decided to have polecat parties in the dining-room. This seemed to involve shredding anything that could be shredded and ripping the stuffing out of all the chairs. More recently they broke into the linen room, where we found the Christmas decorations scattered around the floor as though they had had their Christmas party there. They are not currently my favourite animals, although the Gallinarese smile indulgently whenever they are mentioned. Whatever destruction they cause is excused on the grounds that they are *belle*.

My father was a large, expansive man who loved food, wine, women and Cuban cigars. When he returned to Italy in 1970 he set about reconstructing the house in earnest. Apart from adding bathrooms and redecorating, his major work was the *cantina*. A *cantina* in Italy is a cellar or storeroom for produce and wine. It should be dark, cool and airy. Because our house is built into the side of a hill, the part of the *cantina* that is under the front of the house was quarried into the *tufo*, the volcanic rock upon which Gallinaro is built. It is a grey, porous rock that is prone to weep after heavy rains, keeping the *cantina* humid and cool. The *cantina* runs the length and width of the house and my father enlarged it further, taking it out under the dining-room to the edge of the garden. It is a monument to his life-style — he created for himself and his friends a place designed for and devoted to parties.

It looks almost like a restaurant. At one end there is a bar, and tables and chairs stand around the sides. At the other end there is a small kitchen with a wood-burning range and an enormous spit and griddle, built from local stone. Two stone-arched doorways lead out into the garden, with the same view as from the *terrazza* two storeys above. It is a formal garden, paved with marble, with purpose-built *jardinières* around the sides. Off it is the games room; a sign on the door Reads *'Siate prudenti, l'importuno è sempre in aguato'* – 'Beware, ill-fortune is always lurking'.

Because the *cantina* is such a perfect place for a party, we are forever finding excuses to have one. One of the most memorable was at *carnevale*, or Mardi Gras, in 1986. It started when some friends called to the house on a Friday afternoon.

'Come and see the pig,' they commanded.

I walked with them down to the piazza where a man had a hessian sack. Outraged oinks issued from the sack. A pig in a poke.

'Feel that,' said the man, offering the sack to no one in particular.

'That's a good 40 kilos, that is,' he continued, still holding out the sack. No one took hold of it.

I must have looked bewildered, because my friend Graziano took me aside and explained that this was the pig for the party at *Carnevale* that was to be held in my *cantina* – they would supply the pig, and I would supply the venue. This was the first I'd heard of it, but it sounded like a good idea, since from Graziano's description I had to do nothing for this party other than have fun and get drunk. The deal for the pig was done. It would be delivered to me on Tuesday morning, ready for cooking. I was glad I had not established piggy eye-contact with the beast in the bag, since I rarely enjoy looking food in the eye.

True to their word, a gang turned up on Sunday to prepare the *cantina* for the party. All I had to do was light the fire on Tuesday morning and we would cook the pig on the spit. I had once before cooked a large lamb on a spit, so I felt confident enough about this. The trouble was, I remembered, it had been at a New Year's Eve party in County Offaly in Ireland, where I had spent the day helping my old friend Vincent Slevin keep the fire going and turning the lamb by hand on a crude spit. It took about eight hours to cook and at eleven o'clock at night the drunken revellers descended like vultures on the roast. By the time the scrum cleared Vincent and myself were left looking at a sheep's head and skeleton hanging from the spit. Of our labour not a scrap remained. I promised myself that this would not happen again.

Tuesday morning came and I got up early to start the fire. The woodpile included the remains of a lot of old oak barrels, beautifully seasoned and still smelling of wine. I chose these in the hope that the smell of wine would somehow come through the smoke and flavour the meat, the way apple wood does on a barbecue. Taking wood from the woodpile is something to be done with care and in daylight. Apart from all the normal creepy-crawlies that inhabit woodpiles, it is also home to a large number of scorpions – not the vicious 8-centimetre African variety, just the vicious 4-centimetre Italian variety. Try to sweep them up and they charge the brush like battle-crazed commandos, tails stabbing forward. Their sting isn't fatal, but it does need a doctor.

The spit in the *cantina* is ingeniously designed and overcomes many of the problems of cooking on an open flame. The fire box is not underneath, but at the back of the hearth, held in place by vertical bars. The spit itself is driven by an electric motor and a home-made collection of bicycle gears and chains, and turns in front of the fire rather than above it. To speed up the cooking you can pull embers out from the fire underneath whatever is turning on the spit. The common problem of dripping fat turning the fire into an inferno is avoided by this arrangement and I would recommend it to anyone.

Manœuvring 27 kilos of pig – it weighed less now it was gutted – on to the crossbar of the spit was no simple task. It is important that the weight should be as well balanced as possible or it turns unevenly, making one part over-cooked and leaving another raw. By eleven o'clock the fire was blazing, the burning oak smelt of wine, and the pig was revolving steadily on the spit. Antonio Trionfo arrived. Trionfo is not his surname but his sobriquet. It is common here for everyone to have a nickname, since it helps distinguish one Antonio from another. I know that the surname would serve equally well, but somehow it is never used. Antonio il Biondo, Anthony the Blond, is a typical example, even though anyone used to northern colouring will see nothing blond about him. Anyway, Antonio Trionfo brought bay leaves, seasoning and olive oil. He also showed me a nifty basting technique. As the pig turned he used a sharp knife to cut the skin diagonally all around the roast. He did this in both directions, so that when he'd finished the skin appeared to be tiled with diamonds, about three inches square. When he poured the olive oil on to baste the pig, instead of running straight off it followed the diagonal cuts around and around. He stuffed the inside with bay leaves, wild thyme and mountain oregano. We watched mesmerized as our handiwork turned to the accompanying hum of the electric motor.

It is a feature of any party in Italy that the men will help prepare the food, often more than the women. Italian men love to cook, and the ones I know are very good at it. Even those that aren't are never shy about expressing an opinion. Both the men and the women are critical, not in the sense that they are rude, only that they will comment: 'Mmm, yes, good, but perhaps a little more salt,' or, 'This is an interesting recipe, very tasty, only I've always had it with lemons/capers/ red peppers before, never like this.' If you thought you could get away with missing out an ingredient that the local supermarket had run out of, forget it. They'll spot it at once.

As the day went on the spit's repetitive sound became a kind of chant that was driving me mad: 'I'm turning, *now*

I'm turning – I'm turning, *now* I'm turning,' over and over again. The only interruptions I had were male visitors, each with a culinary opinion or a herb. By six o'clock the pig had started to look and smell very delicious indeed.

We were expecting about thirty people to show up, but numbers are only the vaguest of guesses in Italy. It could easily have been more, but in the event was less. By eight o'clock there were twenty-five people in the *cantina*, almost all of whom had brought several litres of wine. The tremendous rivalry between the producers of wine in Gallinaro often finds expression at parties, when they all bring their finest creation to impress the others. One guest, Antonio Little Fish, had brought a 10-litre demijohn of his cabernet sauvignon. I counted 34 litres in all. I looked at the pig, still turning. 27 kilos of pork for twenty-five people. For a moment I had visions of cold pork sandwiches stretching into the weeks ahead. Someone tried a pig's ear. Being on the outside, they are the first part to cook. It was pronounced excellent. By now the skin of the pig was a golden brown. Encouraged by the success of the ear, we started eating the perfect diamonds of crackling, that had separated slightly, exposing the white fat underneath. Apart from being good to eat, removing these diamonds meant the pork would cook more quickly.

Suddenly there was a commotion. It seemed that no one had thought of bringing bread. Why this should have been a problem given the sheer volume of food on offer was puzzling, but there it was. Someone was dispatched to the bakery and returned with four 2-kilo loaves. It looked to me like waste – surely it would never be eaten? Of course, now I know better. The bread was all eaten, the wine was finished, plus some more that arrived later in the evening, and, as for the pig, it vanished. Only the skull remained, picked clean as though by termites. I have an abiding image of that night of people walking about with huge lumps of pork in their hands. I ate more than I've ever eaten in my life, but was still no match for the trenchermen of Gallinaro.

When it is not in use for parties – that is, most of the time – the *cantina* is a place to go to escape the heat. Because it is almost always kept shut, the air is cool. Sitting there on a summer's afternoon can be bliss. Sunlight streams in through the cracks around the door frames and between the shutters on the windows. The sun is so strong that even these paper-thin shafts of sun are sufficient to light the *cantina*. The contrast between the incoming brightness and the cool of the cellar air is remarkable.

Coming to terms with the heat is part of the acclimatization process. It is not just a question of getting your body used to something it never experiences in Ireland's cool climate, but of learning practical habits that help make the heat bearable. The bedroom windows are only opened in the morning when there is no direct sunlight on them, to air the room. After this they must be shut and the shutters closed. The door, too, must be kept closed so that the hot afternoon air cannot get in. If these habits are not observed, you can end up trying to sleep in a temperature of 30 degrees or more. I find this hard, since once I have cast off the sheet from the bed, there is nothing left to remove. Only a cold shower helps at this point.

Parking the car also needs thought. It's no use leaving it in shade if in twenty minutes it will be in full sun once more. If no shade is available I cover the gear stick and the steering wheel, so I can at least handle them when I return. A car left in the sun can become amazingly hot. I have kept a cassette tape that was left on the passenger seat as a memento. Both the cassette and its case are hideously warped, as though they had been in an oven.

It is important to organize the day with the heat in mind. This means starting car journeys of any length early in the morning, so that you can arrive before eleven o'clock and find some shade. To be stuck on the ring road around Rome at midday in August must be one of the most distressing things that can happen to anyone. How those Romans who remain there in August handle it is a constant source of wonder to me. The heat structures the day for Italians. This is one of the reasons that shops shut between one o'clock and five o'clock; it is uncomfortable to go about one's business in the afternoon heat. The other reason is sleep.

During the summer Gallinaro's social life is like a big party. Everyone knows everyone else and we're all on holiday. The bar stays open to two or three o'clock in the morning and Smeralda's, the night club, blares its music till the early hours. Even when they eventually close, revellers still walk the street, laughing and joking noisily. Because Gallinaro is so small, all this revelry happens under the windows of bedrooms, mine included. On those few nights when we are not ourselves in the street contributing to the racket, going to bed early does not result in sleep. Neither does staying in bed in the morning. By seven o'clock Rafaele is starting his tractor, travelling market-traders drive backwards and forwards through the town, their noisy diesels drowned by the nasty squawk of their roof-mounted loud speakers which inform you of what wares they have on offer. I have never yet felt tempted to leap out of bed at seven o'clock in the morning to buy some salted cod.

By half past seven we are privy to all manner of loud conversations taking place under the bedroom window. Long ago I became convinced that most of Gallinaro's inhabitants were stone deaf, since most conversations are held at the decibel level of a Saturn V take-off and still you hear plenty of 'Eh?'s sprinkling the dialogue. So if you can't sleep at night or in the morning, the afternoon becomes the only time. It works because everyone does it. At one o'clock on the dot the bar empties and the only sound in the alleys of Gallinaro is cutlery on crockery. By two o'clock all you can hear is the song of the cicadas. Traditionally this is also the time to make love to your wife or mistress, although one of the problems of living in a town where the streets are so narrow is that other people's bedrooms are sometimes only a few metres from yours. The last thing you need is someone shouting encouragement to the rhythm of creaking bed-springs.

You can set your watch in Gallinaro either by the church clock, in which case it is always half past ten, or by the movements in the street. After the siesta there is always some movement, but by six o'clock the street is buzzing. The working week for most Italian office workers, including civil servants, is from eight in the morning to two o'clock, six days a week. So, for many people, the time after the siesta is already play-time. Six o'clock is traditionally when the *passeggiata* starts. There is no English equivalent of this, although promenade comes close. The purpose is not to go anywhere or do anything, it is simply to walk round the piazza seeing and being seen. When society was stricter, this was the only time young people got to talk to one another, under the watchful gaze of a chaperone, of course. The morals may have changed, but the patterns of behaviour haven't. The hour between six and seven is for the *passeggiata*. Its purpose is not only for young lovers to meet, but for men to talk business and for women to exchange news. Like the Bar Sinella after Sunday mass, it is a focal point for the day's social exchange, and you can set your watch by its ending. Suddenly at seven o'clock the place is deserted; everyone has gone home to eat. On Sunday the bar is full at quarter to one, the entire village is there, shouting and gesticulating. At one o'clock Sinella clears his tables and gets a chance to sit down and look at the papers. After living in Ireland, where time and space seem to flow seamlessly into one another, this regulation by the clock seems odd. My wife's reaction is always to defy this timetable, but supermarkets, like time and tide, wait for no one. It's pointless to go out to buy food after one o'clock. The shops will be shut and that's the end of it. The only way to survive is to follow the advice of the good Saint Ambrose: when in Rome, follow the Roman rule.

# 4

## *Families and Favours*

It is only in the past few decades that a semblance of stability has come into Italian life. All through the history of the state apparent order has been overturned on seeming caprices of fate. Italians have always known the importance of bending in the wind, of finding a niche where some kind of order can be established. This is the *raison d'être* behind the strength of the family unit. This unit, at least, is in the hands of its members. It can be a bastion against antagonistic influences, whether social or economic. It is axiomatic in Italy that you can trust your family, but you can rarely trust anyone else. This, too, has its effect on the fabric of daily life. Until fairly recently Italians always addressed one another as *lei*, a formal use of the third person singular. We have friends in Rome who, after twenty years in an apartment block, still use *lei* when addressing their neighbour. It is a means of saying, 'We are not close.' For many Italians the step from *lei* to *tu* is still a big one. Although only a verbal convention, moving from one to the other expresses a degree of trust which, although outside the family, is hopefully not misplaced.

Families in Italy are large, not just because there are lots of children, but because they include cousins, second cousins, in-laws, godparents, grandparents, uncles and aunts. Third cousins are aware of one another's presence and, though not strictly obliged to accept one another as family, often do. As a contrast to this, my Irish wife has a first cousin living some six miles from us whom we have seen once in ten years. A small village like mine gives great scope for the *amateur* of genealogy. Given the Italian definition of family, it would be hard to find someone in the village to whom I am not related. Once third cousins by marriage are included, the web stretches far. I learnt as a small boy that when I was taken to Gallinaro, it was prudent to greet everyone that I met as though they were a long-lost intimate. This offended no one, since those who did not consider themselves related were touched, and those who did thought it only natural. My wife has adopted similar tactics and is now much loved for her open and friendly nature.

Italians, despite their apparently carefree life-style, are conservative by nature. They value the past and its lessons, they value order, saving money, education and self-advancement. The family unit makes much of this possible. Family members have the right to call on other members when they need help, but to obtain this right they are also subject to the responsibilities of being a member. Everything is ultimately weighed and balanced. Each favour demands a favour in return, each action is considered before a reaction.

None of this is voiced, but it is as though each person keeps a record of favours given and received. It's no accident that the double-entry accounting system was invented in Italy. This does not mean that there is an immediate return, favour for favour; only that eventually all accounts must be squared. This awareness of balance in all social transactions is universal; even small favours are repaid assiduously. In the Comino Valley, and I am sure over much of Italy, if a friend or relation gives you a plate of freshly made *gnocchi*, you do not return the plate empty. It should be returned with something on it. This tradition is no more than the recognition of the need to keep a balance.

Dinners are a currency in these social transactions. A *cena* is, despite its appearance, a formal mechanism. Dinners become the cement that bonds people and families and it is for this reason that they figure so prominently in daily life. In turn this puts emphasis on food. At any dinner there will always be far too much food. The quantity becomes the measure of the hospitality, which reflects the respect given to the guests. Even the poorest Italians will spend huge sums, almost bankrupting themselves, to produce a wedding feast worthy of their daughter. Weddings, being an overtly formal bonding of two families, produce the most extravagant excesses. Twelve or more courses are not unknown.

I went once with my mother to a wedding where we sat down to eat at one o'clock. We finished our coffee and liqueurs by about half past five. Slowly the guests got to their feet and began to mix. A band played. At around half past six waiters began to clear the tables and reset them. My mother, noticing this, said that it was time we went, since they had clearly arranged for another group of guests to eat dinner with them. We found our hosts to say goodbye.

'My dears, you can't go now, we're just about to have dinner. You really must stay.'

There was no second group. Dinner was for us. This sort of feasting is unusual, but not unknown. Huge meals for huge numbers are the norm for weddings; 300 people would be an average affair. Apart from the food and entertainment, each guest will be given a *bomboniera*, a memento of the wedding, which could range from a net bag of sugared almonds to pieces of silver engraved with the date and the names of the couple. This kind of lavish entertainment imposes obligations on those who accept it. This is why it is so important for a young couple starting off. They begin married life with a deposit book stuffed with favours owing to them.

In the currency of favours smaller change than dinners would be food alone. Someone who makes 20 kilos of sausages when a pig is killed will give some to friends and relations. Should any of them make wine or cheeses, it is reasonable to expect some of that produce in return. In a strictly peasant society this works well enough and balance in these exchanges is usually worked out over the years. The problem comes when you do not deal among equals. Can you give a mayor a kilo of sausages when you need a favour? What if he knows you vote for the opposition?

In these cases only one thing will do the job: *la bustarella*, a little envelope with money in it. This is a vital piece of social grease in Italy. Without it little gets done. If you are not in the position of being able to return a favour to the person of whom you are asking one, then you pay.

This system of favours sets up its own checks and balances on people's behaviour. There is a great uniformity of behaviour among Italians, a high degree of agreement on what is acceptable and what is not. In Ireland eccentricity is the norm. Behaviour that in Ireland would not turn a hair becomes remarkable in Italy. The Italians define themselves very much as part of a group. They refer constantly to *gli amici*, their group of friends and family. Defining themselves as members of a group means that their allegiance to that group is strong. They are mutually supportive. Again, to compare this to Ireland, where no success goes unpunished, in Italy people are proud of members of their group who do well. Into any casual conversation about Britain the subject of Lord Charles Forte will soon come up. Inevitably there is a certain vicarious sharing in his success, a feeling that this success somehow reflects well on the whole valley and its inhabitants. This would never happen in Ireland. You would be regaled instead with stories beginning, 'Sure, I knew him when . . .' which then go on to belittle his achievements. The mutual support that Italians give to one another goes a long way towards explaining their amazing self-confidence.

This is one of the first things visitors to Italy notice. Women in the streets look stunning – they have an air of quiet assurance. Men strut, not thinking, 'My god, I'm beautiful,' but knowing it with a supreme certainty. Children are told from birth that they are beautiful and it makes them thrive. On Italian television game shows, people called on to the stage from the audience are never tongue-tied. They apparently suffer no stage fright and are delighted to be thrust into the limelight. In the summer fat men on beaches lovingly rub oil on to their stomachs with unconscious self-absorption. They appear to like themselves just as they are.

The mutual support, the constant compliments, are cushions around fragile egos. There is no doubt that it gives great strength to the Italians, but it has a down side. Because so many Italians rely on this support from friends and family, they rarely enjoy being alone. In the huge area of wilderness called La Macchiarvana in the Abruzzi, where we go to enjoy winter sports, the vast majority of people will all stick together. On beaches and in the mountains, they gravitate to where everyone else is. This is the complete opposite of Ireland, where in the summer we go to Brittas, on the Wicklow coast. There are lots of little coves, as well as large sandy beaches. We look down from the cliffs and if someone is already there, we go to the next cove. The Italian way would be to ignore the empty beach and join in the fun on the one with people on it.

The family unit also explains why whole villages find themselves displaced to another part of the world. Three times as many people from Casalattico live in Dublin as in the town itself. This is simply because the first to arrive would have sent for his brother and his wife, then her cousin, his cousins, their wives and so on. Anyone thinking of emigrating would always think of going to where family and friends already were. Even my father's decision to leave England and move to Ireland was prompted by his cousin Dino, who lived in Dublin. Like the Irish in America, Italians have family all over Europe, supplying them with a network of connections should they ever need it.

The reliance on family in the modern business world has its drawbacks. Many old-established family firms are in the hands of incompetents, promoted to positions of influence and power solely on the basis of bloodline. The tradition of trusting only the family is a strong one and a display of supreme incompetence would be necessary before an inept family member could be removed. Family businesses in our valley have foundered rather than bring in new blood from outside.

For Italians growing up abroad, family pressure ensured that they married Italians. In my case there was no pressure and I married an Irish girl, but my parents' generation was subject to a lot of coercion. The reason, I think, was that foreigners in general have little idea how an extended Italian family works and first-generation immigrants wanted to make the kind of alliances that they understood.

The ability of Italians to be happy in groups means that high-rise housing does not present the same social problems as it does in other countries. All of Italy's large cities have high-rise apartment blocks. This is partly because land in Italy is scarce and partly because there is no opposition to this form of housing from Italians. Like Hong Kong Chinese, or New Yorkers in Manhattan, this form of housing suits them well.

Italians are house-proud. Their houses are spotlessly clean and scrupulously tidy. It can get carried to extremes. A woman I know in Gallinaro showed me around her house after she had done a great deal of work on it. The kitchen was so immaculate that I wondered out loud how she could cook and have it so clean. She didn't. She showed me her utility kitchen, where she did her cooking, explaining that in this way she could keep her main kitchen spotless. Although extreme, it is not an isolated example. Another family friend in Sora has a master bedroom that she keeps immaculate by the simple expedient of having turned the dressing-room into a bedroom for herself and her husband, thus ensuring the main bedroom doesn't get messed up by actually being used. There is the woman who waits outside the door while guests use the bathroom and who then goes in to disinfect and spray air freshener when they're finished. A cousin of mine puts on specially constructed slippers as soon as he gets home so he can shuffle around the house polishing the parquet as he goes. This insanity is only a physical manifestation of keeping the nub, the centre of the family, in order. The house becomes the public representation of the family's position and aspirations.

It is rare to find among the middle classes in Italy the sort of shabby furnishing so beloved of English country houses. The sofas will not have dog-hairs on them, cats will not sleep undisturbed on an Aga. There is a passion for the new, the shiny, what is *di moda*. Pets until recently were rarely found in Italian houses, mainly I suspect because of their contribution to disorder. A love of beauty is combined with a love of order and to British eyes this may lead an over-emphasis on tidiness and cleanliness in their houses.

Those rare individuals adventurous enough to buy antique furniture will invariably have it polished and restored to the point that all semblance of age is removed. It is also a way of symbolically scrubbing away the touch, the usage of strangers. Italy is a consumer society, where second-hand is not appreciated. I have yet to find an auction room, a car-boot sale or a jumble sale. There is no acceptance of exchanging your old tat for someone else's.

The effort expended on the interior does not always extend to the outside of the house. When I was about eleven my mother took me to visit a school-friend of hers who lived in Arpino. Through a dingy courtyard we approached what looked to me like a crumbling, run-down *palazzo*; in my experience such buildings were known as tenements. As soon as the front door opened my preconceptions were rudely destroyed. Downstairs beautiful marble floors gleamed, while upstairs on the *piano nobile* sixteenth-century parquet of great beauty gleamed beneath centuries of beeswax. Exquisite paintings hung on the panelled walls, while we sat and took tea on furniture from the *settecento*. Old money in Italy has a way of lying low. It is never flaunted. Indeed in recent years it has become dangerous to display wealth. Kidnapping is sufficiently common now that it touched good friends of my mother's in 1991, when their grandson was kidnapped. Thankfully the child was unharmed, but their house on the Via Appia Antica now resembles a prison, in an attempt to be impregnable. The only way you can drive a Ferrari safely today is if you wear mechanic's overalls.

The obsession with cleanliness and order doesn't only apply to houses. Italians bring this obsession to personal hygiene. Hoteliers that I know in Ireland hate having Italians to stay. They use lots of hot water, they are constantly asking for clean towels. But this is their habit. Next to any lavatory bowl in Italy there is a bidet. It is not considered a luxury but a necessity. Sheets are commonly washed and ironed daily, even the heavy linen ones. On a crowded commuter train in Rome, even in summer, you can smell soap and cologne.

Self-improvement is a concept that Italians revere. Rural Italy has for years been class-ridden, with the peasants kept in their place by lack of education. Local lore is full of stories of poor men who have been *fregato* – conned – simply because they couldn't read a contract or fill in a government form. They were treated as fools by officials, whether in government offices or in banks, so literacy and education became a Holy Grail. Only through education was self-improvement a possibility, only education or emigration offered a way out from the grind of working the land. This aspiration has been fulfilled by the modern Italian post-war republic.

The drive for literacy and education among people who were traditionally without has produced some extraordinary stories. While my father was at university in Florence, he met a young man from the Comino Valley called Vittorio Grimaldi. In 1942 Vittorio went to Florence to enrol. Not being able to afford a train, he decided to go on his bicycle, which had rags tied around the wheels instead of tyres. Florence is about 300 miles away. His mother equipped him for this journey with some rolls, and trousers made from an old sheet, which she had dyed black. By mid-journey his rolls were long finished, he was hungry and tired. A farm worker saw him on the road and invited him to eat with him that night. The menu was *polenta*.

Maize meal has been a staple of the Italian diet for centuries. It was used for animal feed, for *polenta* and for bread. Like hominy grits, *polenta* is maize semolina boiled to a consistency of thick porridge, which is then spread out on a platter and eaten with butter, gravy or *ragù* − a tomato sauce. It is traditional to pour the *polenta* on to a board, cover it with *ragù* and then place the sausages that flavoured the sauce in the middle of the *polenta*. At the 'go' signal, the end of grace, the race begins. Each diner begins eating from the edge nearest their place. Whoever gets to the middle first gets the sausages.

For the family Vittorio stayed with that night there was no contest: he was like a ravenous wolf, eating most of the *polenta* and all of the sausages. He eventually arrived in Florence for his interview. It had been raining hard and as he sat in the interview room a black puddle began to form as the dye ran out of his trousers. He was uncomfortable and embarrassed. He didn't do very well in the interview and when it was over one last question was asked.

'How did you get here?'

'By bike.'

'No, I mean here to Florence.'

'By bike.'

There was a stunned silence, broken by one of the professors who said that anyone prepared to make a journey like that deserved a place. And deserve it he did, finishing his final year as a vet with the highest marks in all Italy that year, graduating *magna cum laude*.

Today schooling is available free for everyone. From the age of three children can go to the *nido* – literally a nest – which is a pre-school playgroup. It also serves as a crèche, allowing Italian women to work. Even in a village like Gallinaro there is a communal bus, which collects children from every house, takes them to school and returns them afterwards to the door. No matter how isolated a house, the bus comes for the children. So good have the state schools become that private schools have virtually ceased to exist. Many of those that do exist are only for the educationally sub-normal, rather than for the privileged. If you were to tell someone that your child goes to a private school, the most likely response would be sympathetic.

Third-level education is encouraged, and a pupil who has passed the baccalaureate has the right to go the university of their choice to study the subject of their choice. This law poses some problems for the universities. If 4,000 applications arrive one year for the faculty of medicine in the University of Rome, the faculty must accommodate all of them. Obviously this puts strains on the teaching staff as well as filling lecture halls far beyond their designed capacity. It has also caused over the years a glut of graduates in some professions, who now have enormous difficulty finding work. Of the fourteen males within five years of my age in Gallinaro two have higher-level diplomas, the rest university degrees. Five are doctors who, luckily, have work.

If these statistics were national, the results would be extra-ordinary. In rural Frosinone there is a drive to ensure that offspring study hard and earn degrees, a direct response to the historical lack of education. Families prod and cajole their children to study hard, at school and at home, in term time and throughout the holidays. The result is a valley of well-qualified people who unfortunately cannot always find work in their chosen profession. One of my friends, with a degree in jurisprudence, drove the school bus for years. Recently the universities have responded by making their courses harder to complete. The drop-out rate in the first year or two is high, so that graduate numbers are now coming into line with what the market needs.

In situations like this young graduates have only their family to fall back on. Most jobs in Italy are obtained by recommendation – that is, the family recommends the applicant to someone who is a friend, or who owes a favour. For many years it has been possible to influence the outcome of an exam, since a list of the examiners is published. The examiners can then be approached and persuaded that a particular candidate should not be failed. Many degrees have been obtained by this means, ensuring that in various professions some extraordinarily inept people find gainful employment.

Until very recently the easiest way to earn a basic crust was to become an invalid. There are over one million official invalids in Italy, all of whom get assistance from the state of roughly £500 a month. All that was needed was pliant town councillors, who would fill in the necessary forms in return for a vote. The little village of Militello Rosmarino in Sicily has become famous since the news of its huge invalid population hit the media. Out of its population of 1,200 citizens, 500 are invalids. Investigators have discovered centre-forwards who are cripples and bus-drivers who are blind.

The family unit provides its members with many necessities throughout life, and especially towards the end of it. Old people rarely go to homes for the elderly; they live in the family house with everyone else. The law underpins this system: it is not possible for a man to leave his house on his death to anyone other than his wife unless she is given the right to live in the house until her death. Although King Lear doesn't figure largely in local folklore, it is rare for anyone to bequeath what they have to relations before their death. The hope of an inheritance is used as a kind of insurance policy by the elderly to ensure that they are never left unattended or homeless.

Because so much of life is organized through the family, the concept of owing your allegiance to a particular group within society is easily understood. If times are hard and government oppressive, it is a small step from here to a larger family such as the Mafia or the Camorra. Originally, Sicilians banded together in self-defence, to protect their families and crops against rapacious landlords or brigands. When large numbers of Italians found themselves in America, far from home and family, not speaking the language, the Mafia became an ersatz family that worked by the same conventions of favours bequeathed and owed, and offered much the same protection from a hostile environment. The web of connections that was offered by allegiance to the Mafia ensured protection from other racketeers, respect for the old, and jobs.

The New York branches are called 'families', even though bloodline has little to do with membership. Mafia Dons like to see themselves as a paterfamilias, correcting wayward family members for the good of the group, and dispensing favours and largesse when deserved. Oddly, the idea of a paterfamilias holding the right of life and death over the members of his family goes back to Roman law. Whatever else may be said about the Mafia, it does demonstrate that, when it matters, Italians are prepared to accept discipline. The Mafia and the Camorra are both disciplined groups, rigidly ordered and brutally policed. The loose grouping that is the government, consisting of deputies who owe no allegiance to one another, who share no common bond other than fear of exposure, is no match for the order of organized crime. By comparison, Italian government at all levels from local to national seems both venal and weak, its own self-interest taking precedence over all other considerations. The rapid post-war growth of the Mafia is testament to this.

# 5

## *Difficult is Best*

Italians are not generally morose, dispassionate and introspective. They are animated, extrovert and, above all, extreme. Their obsession with taking things to extremes is, I must admit, something that I have only recently noticed. It is their extreme behaviour when dealing with food that set me thinking. The twelve-course banquets of which they are so fond are only the tip of an iceberg of immoderation.

When I was in my late teens I spent the summers in Italy. My friends and cousins at that time had just become mobile, largely thanks to the *Cinquecento*, the Fiat 500. Whole days were spent cruising with the roof open looking for something to do, or preferably people with breasts. Nobody had a factory specification *Cinquecento* – each car was unique, either because of imaginative paintwork, or because of imaginative engineering. Many different *Cinquecenti* were made by the coachwork factories of the North – Giannini, Abarth and Autobianchi – who all put non-standard bodies on the Fiat running gear. They were tuned, tweaked and persuaded to exceed the 90 kilometres an hour they were designed to do. They were fitted with air-horns and exhausts tuned to make them sound like a Formula 1. Designed to be admired, they were flaunted and paraded.

Excuses to go somewhere were invented for the flimsiest of reasons, or so I thought. It was not uncommon to drive 30 kilometres past dozens of *bar-gelaterie* to find a particular *gelateria* where the ice-cream was said to be infinitely superior to anywhere else. This held true for coffee as well. In the whole of Sora there was no coffee to compare with that in Isola Liri. I was convinced that all the cars we passed on the road to Isola were on their way to Sora, equally convinced that coffee could only be drunk in Sora. I could never detect any difference in coffee or ice-cream that could have justified so long a drive.

I remember several occasions when I was driven nearly 60 kilometres for a pizza. Needless to say, this was pizza the like of which was unobtainable anywhere else. It merited the drive, the expenditure of time, of petrol. I could never spot the subtle differences that prompted these journeys. And yet, when I thought about it, the only difference a car made was to increase the travelling distance. Even on foot Italians behave in the same way. It is very common to be roused from a dinner-table in a restaurant to walk elsewhere for coffee or ice-cream, normally just as you're getting comfortable. The entire company will be agreeing that coffee in the Bar Roma three blocks away is the only way to round off a meal.

I am now convinced that all this movement has its purpose. It adds colour to the evening and it adds variety. More importantly, though, it is a manifestation of Italian discrimination. With food and drink, discrimination is the Shangri-La to which all Italians aspire. To be able to tell by taste alone whether a pizza has been cooked in a brick oven using vine thinnings or by some other form of firing is impressive. Being able to discover the bar that serves the best coffee marks the discoverer as a man who values the good things in life, and who takes the time and trouble to source them.

The ability to see subtle distinctions is a gift that all Italians have, mainly because it's something they practise. On a hot August night we sat after dinner with our old friends Wanda and Memmo Regoli in their house in Arpino.

'Let's sit on the balcony,' suggested Memmo.

The house is large, and all the windows that look on to the street have balconies. As I settled myself, looking over Arpino by night, my host insisted on moving again.

'The air on the study balcony is cooler.'

We moved to the study. The air quality seemed exactly the same to me.

'Now, that's better, isn't it?'

I mumbled assent.

'Tell you what – upstairs it's even better. Come on.'

Upstairs, we tried the balconies of all the bedrooms.

'See how the air moves differently?'

I didn't, but agreed anyway. The balconies were at most 3 metres apart – the subtlety of discrimination needed to notice a difference was beyond me.

Can they really tell? I honestly don't know, but everyone behaves as though they do. Shades and nuances are remarked upon, noted and discussed. I have been taken to see a field which was no more than a quarter acre, and had explained to me how the land produced different flavours of vegetables depending on where they were planted. Had it been a 30-acre field with varying soil types, I would have found it easier to believe. And yet it might be true. Vine-growers have always known that grapes develop differently in different parts of the vineyard.

The idea that discrimination is possible even in minutiae leads to interesting behaviour. Apart from travelling miles to seek out the best coffee, the inhabitants of the big cities will travel miles into the countryside to buy eggs, olive oil, cheeses and wine from local producers. The guiding principle in all this is whether or not the food is *genuino*. Food scandals are second in quantity only to political scandals. Some years ago there was a popular table wine called Vino Ferrari. It was cheap and pleasant to drink. It was sold all over Italy until someone with acute powers of observation noticed that for all

the thousands of lorries leaving the factory full of wine, not one laden with grapes ever went in. The wine was made with industrial alcohol, colourings and flavourings. Over the years there have been rumours of margarine made from spent sump oil, olive oil made from everything except olives, endless adulterants in commercial wine and tinned meat of doubtful origins. Not surprisingly, Italians have little confidence in the labels listing the contents of what they buy.

This is why a trip to the country at the weekends always includes food stops. Many of the inhabitants of Italy's large cities have relations in the country. There is a widespread belief that produce bought locally is somehow more genuine. Being Italy this trust is not always well placed, as there are examples of farmers buying eggs from battery farms and then selling them, properly covered in dung, to the seekers of *il genuino*. Yet, despite occasional lapses, buyers are more likely to obtain real food in this way than they are in a supermarket.

Even people who live in the country will travel for certain things. The tiny hamlets at the upper edges of the Comino Valley, like Fondillo or Forestelle, are home to shepherds whose flocks graze the upper reaches of the Apennines. Until recently, the roads to these hamlets were unsurfaced and distinctly dangerous. This did not prevent people from going there to buy the highly rated sheep's cheeses made by the shepherds' wives. *Pecorino, caciotta* and *ricotta*, all basic ingredients of Italian cuisine, are most prized when bought on the spot. There is little doubt that cheeses like these, certainly breaking every diktat from Strasbourg on the production of cheese, have a taste second to none. What I find surprising is not that the home-made is preferable to the industrial substitute, but that Italians recognize this and are prepared to endure uncomfortable drives to obtain it.

Above Picinisco lie the Prati di Mezzo, high pastures that in the summer are cool and breezy. There is a stream running through the pastures fed by mountain springs that are clear and cold. It's one of our favourite picnic spots, since it's never too hot and ice-cold water is always available. The only sound up here other than birdsong is the dull clanging of the bells around the necks of horses and creamy-white cows brought to the mountains to graze. We often see Italian families carrying plastic bags, which, if they are lucky, are filled with mountain asparagus. These tiny, thin, slightly bitter spears are tedious to collect. Yet the urge for vegetables that are unsprayed and unforced takes people to the hills in droves.

The same urge results in foraging for alpine strawberries, tiny, perfumed fruits with a taste like nectar. These are normally made into liqueur, rather than eaten as dessert. But the foraging instinct reaches its most sophisticated when it comes to truffles.

In the upper reaches of the western end of the Comino Valley is the town of Campoli. Many of its inhabitants make their living wholly or in part from collecting truffles on the lower Apennine slopes. What grows in Campoli in greater abundance than elsewhere in the valley are black truffles, the *tuber aestivum*. This is not the famed truffle of Périgord, but it can at certain times of the year fetch £250 a kilo, enough to make even an average day pay fairly well. Truffle-hunters have clearly defined areas for foraging, not officially, but traditionally. They are handed down from father to son and the right to these areas is mutually respected by the truffle-gatherers. Casual truffle-hunters in these hills are likely to run into angry men with dogs and guns, jealous of their territory. Although Campoli is renowned for an abundance of truffles, they do grow in the valley proper, even where I have land on Monte Cicuto. There is one permanent resident on Monte Cicuto, who lives in a small-holding right at the very top. His name is Egidio and he is known throughout the valley as an incomparable jack of all trades.

Apart from being a fine chef, importing smoked salmon from Ireland and selling firewood, he also collects truffles. To find truffles you need the help of better olfactory equipment than the human being is provided with. Pigs are used to root them out, but dogs are more commonly used in the valley. Training a dog to hunt for truffles is easy enough. You feed your puppy truffles with all its meals, so before long it associates food with truffles. When it is grown, you attach a strong choke chain to its neck and take it to your truffle grounds. The dog at once starts to sniff out its intended snack and as soon as it starts to dig, you pull hard on the choke chain, take the unearthed truffles and give the dog a truffle-flavoured biscuit by way of consolation. Pigs are better than dogs at sniffing out truffles, but are harder to pull back when they have found some and less pleased than a dog to accept a substitute.

One year I had been given a lot of truffles and I decided that my fortune could be made by training my Irish labrador to become a truffle-hound. I packed a large storage jar with truffles surrounded with rice to keep them fresh and brought them back to Wicklow. Carefully I chopped them into a bowl for my dog. She, equally carefully, chewed a large mouthful and then spat it back into the bowl. And so it was that eight fine truffles went into the bin, and I have yet to own a truffle-hound.

My old friend Nicola Celestino is a doctor who has a clinic three days a week in Campoli. Over the years grateful patients have given him the usual quota of eggs, oil, wine and sausages, but, being in Campoli, he is also regularly given truffles. Like the dogs, he now has an insatiable appetite for them. Nicola travels more than anyone else I know, seven or eight trips a year all over the globe. On a trip to Czechoslovakia he was walking through a forest chatting to the locals. He talked of truffles. They told him the forests were full of them, but that no one collected them or had any use for them. That's a bit like telling an Irishman they're serving free beer down at the pub. As soon as he got home he went to see Egidio. They planned a November trip by car to Czechoslovakia with the dogs.

Came the day, and Nicola phoned Egidio to make arrangements for picking him up.

'I haven't much cash with me,' said Egidio.

'Don't worry,' Nicola replied, 'I've probably got enough for both of us.'

Egidio collected Nicola in his old van and they picked up the *autostrada* at Frosinone. After some 20 kilometres Egidio suggested they stop for coffee. He insisted on paying for the coffees, and when they were back in the car he announced, 'Well, that's me cleaned out.'

As it happened, Nicola had enough to get them there and back. What Nicola remembers best of this trip is the flies. Whatever Egidio had been keeping in his van had attracted flies – lots of them. Nicola swears he didn't manage to get the last one out of the van until they reached Vienna. Unfortunately winter arrives early in the mountain forests of Czechoslovakia and 45 centimetres of ground frost foiled their attempts at truffle-hunting. Five days later they were home, empty-handed.

For years I was ambivalent about truffles. Sometimes we were treated to truffle spaghetti or rice, but I could never really see what the fuss was about. It was good, but not good enough to go out of your way for. But then in 1992 I had Nicola's truffle salad. The ingredients are simple: 1 kilo of truffles and 1 kilo of fresh parmesan, both coarsely grated and mixed in a bowl with good extra-virgin olive oil. Now I know: truffle love is to do with quantity. A little grated reverentially on top of a bowl of rice is meaningless – it's a sop to culinary snobs. But Nicola's salad is an epicure's dream, simple and stunningly good. My advice is clear: don't bother with truffles unless you can eat a lot of them.

Not all of Nicola's dealings with Egidio have been disasters. Johnny the Boar turned out well. It happened like this. Some hunters were shooting wild boar in the valley and had found a male piglet which they gave to Nicola. Nicola took it to Egidio, who fed and fattened it and christened it Johnny. By the following winter, Johnny weighed in at close to 400 kilos – a monster. Just like real eggs or real olive oil, a boar that has been allowed to root for tubers, and eat acorns and maize rather than a factory-bred pig's diet, is a prized possession. And

400 kilos is a lot of genuine pork. Johnny the Boar was what is known as a *ruspante* pig, one that is allowed to forage free range, and as such commands a hefty premium over the ordinary variety.

In the valley battery chickens are rare, though they are becoming commoner with the advent of large supermarkets. There is still a widely held belief that eating battery chickens makes you impotent, a fate worse than death for any Italian male. Chickens are sold in the markets, often still squawking, or in butchers' shops with head and feet still attached. This gives the buyer a chance to look for the tell-tale signs of battery provenance. Long, thin legs are preferred to short fat ones, since they are a sure sign of a chicken that has done some walking.

All foods are sought out in as close to their natural state as is possible. Pasta is a staple, but Italians would crawl over broken glass for a good plateful of pasta *fatta in casa*, the home-made variety. All Italian cookery is labour-intensive and home-made pasta is no exception. It is hard work mixing the flour with the eggs, it's harder still to keep working and rolling it with a broom handle until it becomes like silk. Then it has to be rolled out and cut by hand, either into thin strips for *tagliatelle*, or into larger rectangles for *cannelloni*. It is the effort as much as the taste that is appreciated. Most people have little time for short cuts. Some years ago I bought a remarkable machine called a Pastamatic. You put flour and eggs into a container, switch it on, and after a while out comes your fresh pasta in any shape you desire, including the tubular forms. Not one of my friends was impressed. While accepting that the product was *like* real pasta, it couldn't possibly taste right since it hadn't been rolled by hand. About the only device that is permissible is a *chitarra* – a wooden frame across which fine wire is stretched taut, hence its name, meaning 'guitar'. The thin sheets of fresh pasta are placed on the *chitarra*, and then the rolling-pin passed over it, slicing the pasta into strips. Anything that makes life any easier than this is suspect.

Just as making pasta needs to be difficult to be good, so does preparing the tomatoes that make a lot of the pasta sauces. *Passata*, or sieved tomatoes, is easily bought in bottles or tins, but few people in the valley will use the bought variety. In July and August you can see in the courtyards of the houses huge cauldrons on bonfires. It's tomato time again. They are boiled, skinned and put into preserving jars. More often than not preserving jars with wide tops are not used. It's too easy that way. Traditionally we have always used 1-litre beer bottles – the ones with a narrow neck. Each member of the team has a small stick, about the size of a pencil, and each tomato – the plum variety – is pushed into the beer bottle with the stick: slowly. I have helped perform this operation with 90 kilos of tomatoes, all going into beer bottles. The theory, as always, is that it can't be good unless it's difficult. The narrow necks of the crown-capped beer bottles ensures that air has a slim chance of entering and spoiling the tomatoes. Personally, I'd rather lose the odd tomato to mould than fill another beer bottle.

So ingrained is this idea that it turns up in jokes. One of

the simplest pasta sauces is *aglio e olio*, olive oil warmed with some garlic and optionally some chilli. If a wife presents this to her spouse at lunchtime it is called *pasto del cornuto*, cuckold's lunch, since it takes so little time to prepare that the wife could have spent the morning with her lover. This would clearly be impossible, even for a superwoman, if home-made *tagliatelle* were on the menu.

There is a widespread distrust of any commercially produced foods. I long ago discovered that by offering my friends in Gallinaro a glass of commercially produced wine, I would first get sympathy for having to drink such an unpalatable liquid, and then I'd be given few litres of the real stuff. I remember once testing out how far this prejudice would go by taking to Italy a couple of bottles of Château Malescot St Exupéry 1970 and having it with supper. The effect was the same. Don't care what it costs, it's pasteurized and filtered, probably adulterated and not worth having. The Comino Valley has always been a wine-producing area, but the science of making wine for laying down is neither understood nor appreciated. Wine is made in the autumn for next year's consumption. It is made to be drunk young, and does not last well. The taste of young, unpasteurized, unfiltered wine is very different from the taste of a classic claret. But when it is good, it is nectar.

The old theory that difficult is best applies to making wine as well. For years wine-making in Gallinaro followed the same ritual: the crushed grapes were tipped into the fermenting barrel and then, fermentation over, it was racked off into 50-litre demijohns. This means over the course of the year a lot of humping, heaving and sterilizing heavy glass demijohns. Nicola is almost alone in using the new fibreglass containers that hold 1,000 litres and dispense with twenty demijohns. The local experts claim they can detect a taste of resin in the wine. The old, hard way is best.

Much of the time spent during the day is devoted to food,

not just preparing it, but buying it. Watch an Italian woman buying fruit. She will not even contemplate picking up a kilo-bag of oranges. She will pick oranges from a pile, one at a time, squeeze each one, check for blemishes and slowly put together her choice. This is repeated for all the vegetables that she needs. Everything is examined minutely; only produce that fits her exacting standards will be bought. Time spent in selection is not considered time wasted.

Huge bakeries with fleets of vans supplying bread for an 80-kilometre radius are unheard of. Even tiny villages have their own bakery, so that fresh bread can be bought twice a day. Italian bread has the same property as French bread – it goes hard quickly – so supplies are bought little and often. Despite the fact that there is a bakery in every village, people still travel to find the best bread. There is a bakery in Ponte Melfa known as Cesinella which has a permanent queue. People from villages at the other end of valley come here to buy bread and pizza, passing four or five bakeries on the way.

Living in Ireland, where fish is plentiful, cheap and almost completely unappreciated, I find the Italian attitude to fish remarkable. In Italy fish is a treat, a special food for special occasions and not a penance for Fridays. It is also expensive; a meal in a restaurant will double in price when fish is served. For an honoured guest at dinner the menu will certainly contain fish, or will be entirely composed of it. Again, time and trouble are no obstacle when it comes to obtaining it. Although it can be bought frozen in supermarkets or fresh in the markets, it is not unusual for people in the valley to drive to Formia or Gaeta, a 130-kilometre round trip, to buy their fish at the quayside. Nobody considers this exceptional or extreme behaviour. How else can you be sure the fish is as fresh as possible?

What it all comes down to is that Italians believe food is important. It is discussed as endlessly as the English discuss the weather. It is the one sensory pleasure that can be enjoyed several times a day, right up to their demise.

There is one concept that Italians apply to food that sets them apart from many other races – the idea of a larder, a *cantina*. When my friend Graziano was a student living in a bedsit in Rome, I would see him only at weekends. One day he was extolling the virtues of *bagna cauda*, a tasty but difficult pasta sauce that takes a bit of preparation. I voiced my surprise that a student living on his own would take so much trouble to make a meal for himself. No, no, no, I was missing the point. You don't make *la bagna cauda* each time you fancy it; you make a couple of kilos one afternoon and put it in the storeroom. From then on, you have a quick and easy snack available. The penny dropped. That's why you spend a day making sausages for the year ahead, why the tomatoes are bottled in such quantity.

One of the great delights of summer in Gallinaro is the endless round of dinners and parties. Many of these evenings, and also evenings spent in Sinella's bar, end up in someone's *cantina* in the early hours. I've always associated midnight snacks with school dormitories, but in Gallinaro during the summer they are nightly occurrences. If you have anything planned for the next day, they are best avoided. On at least two occasions I have been carried home, fruity cabernet sauvignon having caught me unawares. Demijohns of wine are decanted, the *prosciutto* is brought out, the *salsicce* are produced, cheeses are sliced. No preparation is necessary – all you need is bread. The delights of an Italian country kitchen are instantly available for sharing with friends. It's surprising, but even when I was not hungry, I have been able to eat as much as anyone else. The salty hams, sausages and cheeses bring on a thirst, which can only be slaked by more wine. As ever, good times in Italy mean plenty of wine and plenty of real, genuine food.

A well-stocked *cantina* will be stuffed with fruit, root

vegetables, nuts and mushrooms, all gathered in their due season and stored for later consumption. There will be sausages and *prosciutti* hanging from the ceiling, and little wicker baskets that are the traditional moulds for the curd cheeses and *ricotta*. Mushrooms, although lower in the pecking-order than truffles, are prized. Nearly everyone knows the main varieties and nearly everyone goes out to gather them. Italians will tell you that mushrooms only last a day. And in Italy this is true, not because it's the life-span of the fungus, but because as soon as they pop their heads out of the ground there will be an Italian there to pick them. You really do have to get up early in the morning to gather mushrooms, because if you don't, someone else will get there first. The contrast with Ireland is dramatic. In Ireland mushrooms are not gathered, but are left to complete their natural cycle. I have watched ceps growing in roadside verges which over a week matured to 500 or 600 grammes, which is when I picked them. *Porcini*, or ceps, the *boletus edulis*, are the most prized. They are easily dried and can be reconstituted in water at a later stage, making them ideal candidates for the *cantina*.

The pre-occupation with good, genuine food, unadulterated and natural, prompts one of Italy's best-known excesses: shooting. Anyone with a love of songbirds will find the Italian habit of eating them hard to accept. I suspect that, given a wide array of game to kill, the average Italian hunter would not necessarily take songbirds as first choice, but since anything larger than this has long been eradicated from Italic shores, they'll do. If roast pheasant is out of the question, then thrush it will have to be.

I am told that in Italy there are ten million licensed guns. That's a fair chunk of the adult population, and of the male adults, it must be well over half. Attempts by government to control shooting founder on this block of votes. The Italian gun licence is an interesting creature. It applies not to the weapon, but to the user, so one licence means as many guns as you like, providing they are of the same calibre. A rifle requires a separate licence from a shotgun, but apart from this limitation a licence validates any number of guns within its category. The other oddity of the Italian gun licence is that it gives the holder the right to walk on any part of Italian territory – even someone's back garden. This rests on the established precept of Italian law that all land is ultimately vested in the state, therefore the state can give permission for its lands to be walked. Nowhere is inviolate, although some areas are being preserved as game sanctuaries.

Some animals have re-established themselves surprisingly well despite the hunting. Because many of the workers in the Comino Valley now work in industry, and many have emigrated, much of the land which was once cultivated with vines or olives is now abandoned. This suits the wild boar well – there is cover, less human contact, and food in abundance. At night on my *terrazza* we can hear their muffled grunts in the valley below.

Shooting birds has become so pervasive that one of the first things a visitor to the Italian countryside notices is the lack of birdsong. Gallinaro still has its share of inedible birds – swallows and owls – but little else. Already there have been referenda to attempt to curtail shooting, but so far to no avail. What gives me hope for the wildlife is the characteristic extreme behaviour of the Italians. About ten years ago, especially after the winter floods, rivers and streams had borders of a remarkable fruit – nearly every overhanging branch, up to the level of high water, was covered with plastic bags. They had become so ubiquitous, and Italians so lax at disposing of them, that the state of the rivers became a scandal. The eventual reaction was equally extreme. Italy became one of the first countries to insist upon biodegradable plastic bags, and it seems to have worked. It is my guess that when awareness of the lack of songbirds becomes general, Italy will introduce the most stringently controlled shooting in Europe.

To take another example, when my son was a baby we would go from shop to shop looking for baby food that was not full of sugar. Eventually we discovered that it was available in chemist shops in the diabetic section. We were considered odd, cranky, for limiting his sugar intake, but now, *en masse*, the Italians have gone the same way. Now you can't find baby food with added sugar anywhere.

It seems the middle road is not one Italians will take. They like extremes, in all aspects of their life, including politics. They embraced fascism whole-heartedly and rejected it equally whole-heartedly. Nothing comes in moderation, least of all moderation.

# 6

## *Naples and the Law*

Although prior to the founding of the modern Italian state the Comino Valley was part of the Kingdom of Naples, culturally its links have always been with Rome. The reasons for this are partly geographical – it was easier to get to Rome – and partly historical, since the valley was one of the first regions to come under Roman dominance in the first millennium BC; Arpino, which borders the valley, was the birthplace of Marcus Tullius Cicero, Agrippa and Caius Marius. It was the first city to be granted the right of Roman citizenship, which amongst other things conferred preferential trading rights. After the Roman defeat of the Samnites the valley became part of the Roman Adiectum, and Atina, the largest of the valley towns, become a *praefectura*.

The influence of Naples is still felt, however. Tales are told of Francesco, the last king of Naples, loved by his subjects since he spoke only Neapolitan, and never Italian. As soon as you leave our valley and go to Cassino, Naples seems much closer. The manner of the shopkeepers, the dialect, even the flora, become similar to those of Campania, the region centred on Naples. A casual visitor may not spot these likenesses, but even the least observant will notice that the nearer you get to Naples, the better the coffee tastes. This curious phenomenon is confirmed even by many who dislike Naples and Neapolitans. Quite why coffee should taste ambrosial in Naples is anyone's guess. Personally, I think it's the water.

It's hard to be indifferent to Naples. It arouses strong feelings among Italians, who either, like me, are in love with it, or hate all that it represents. Certainly the street markets are more like souks than their European counterparts. The streets are narrow, crowded and noisy, washing hangs across them like bunting. There is a vibrancy in the air that is hard to pin down.

There are many myths about Naples: it is violent, you'll get ripped off, they're all on the dole, every sweatshop in Italy is here, it's lawless, the people are feckless, and so on. There is a grain of truth in all of this, but it comes nowhere close to describing Naples.

As soon as you get to the end of the motorway to Naples, there are hawkers selling bootleg tapes and all manner of gee-gaws to contend with. It is the opening salvo in the city's attempt to part you from your money. You may not be in the market for contraband diamonds or cigarettes stolen from the American PX stores, but anyone with something to sell will seek you out. At a garage on the outskirts I was singled out at once – a car with foreign number plates has much the same effect on Neapolitans as honey has on bees – and in no time I was offered from the boot of a car a video recorder, a camcorder and a television. The fact that I only had the equivalent of £50 on me did not deter the salesmen.

'Just the video then,' they said.

I wasn't quite sure I'd heard correctly. 'I've only got 100,000 lire.'

'Well, just buy the recorder, then,' they repeated, pointing to one of the boxes in the boot of the car.

Through the shrink-wrap, on which the guarantee was sellotaped, I could see from the box that it was the latest model from JVC. I reached into my pocket, greedy and eager. Then I remembered that my wife, who was sitting filing her nails in the car, had the money. I walked over to our car, a hustler in tow. He showed the box to my wife.

79

As she continued filing she turned to me and asked, 'Have you seen what's inside the box?'

I hadn't.

Meanwhile, on the pretext that hanging around a garage forecourt with hot goods was bad for his health, my new-found friend continued to press me. 'I have to sell this lot quick. I have to get to Sicily. I'm selling cheap for a quick sale. Come on, what's 100,000 lire? It's a giveaway.'

'Can you open the box and let me have a look at it?'

He took the box and went back to his car, which I noticed had Neapolitan plates. Thank God my wife does not have her head turned as easily as I do. *Caveat emptor* is a phrase to keep in mind in Naples.

When we got home I started to tell the story to a friend.

'My God,' he interrupted, 'you didn't buy it, did you? A box of bricks would be expensive at 100,000 lire.'

Anyone could tell you a similar tale. Some end well, like mine; others with further embarrassment when the bricks are paid for and unwrapped at home before an expectant audience. Oddly enough, I have yet to be done in Naples and so have nothing but love for the place. Dealing with the hawkers is not hard really. The Neapolitans are extraordinarily polite and will for the most part take a polite refusal as long as your voice carries no uncertainty. A smell of indecision will keep them on your tail for two blocks.

My uncle once told me of how he'd been offered 'gold' bracelets in Naples. He looked at the bangles appreciatively, and asked: 'How much are they a kilo?'

The seller was a little taken aback.

'Well,' my uncle continued, 'you surely don't sell them individually?'

The seller stepped back, and wrapped up his wares. '*Come non fu detto* [as if nothing has been said], *dottore*,' and left.

Naples is a city of hustlers and they learn young. At most traffic-lights in the city, you will be accosted by urchins who want to wash your windscreen, sell you tissues or disposable lighters, or all three. That is, if you are allowed to stop at red traffic-lights. I stopped at them once, and nearly got rammed from behind. Angry Neapolitans passed me on both my right and my left, cursing and gesticulating. Driving here is a bit like fairground dodgems and the rules seem to be about the same. Certainly, it's the only I city I know where traffic-lights are universally ignored. I was once driving a friend who lives just outside Naples through Rome. When I stopped at some traffic-lights along with the rest of the traffic, he turned to me and said, 'They're very disciplined drivers up here, aren't they?'

If I were hungry, let me be hungry in Naples. I have walked down narrow alleys and passed someone on their doorstep eating spaghetti and have been offered some. It is still the custom here to offer to share your food with anyone who passes while you might be eating. '*Favorisci?*' – 'Would you like some?' There is a solidarity in centuries of poverty, a common thread that joins the people against the vagaries of fortune and government. Neapolitans know the art of *arrangiarsi*, making the best of what you have. They are quick, flexible and cunning. They are proud, honourable and ethical by their rules. You are unlikely to be mugged in Naples – in Rome, yes, but not in Naples. Here they will part a fool and his money with alarming rapidity, but not through violence. Their weapon is cunning and adaptability. One smart hustler is currently working the traffic jams with a cellular phone. He'll let you make a call from your car for 5,000 lire. For someone who could easily be stuck for two or three hours, that's a real service. The day the new law came into effect making seat-belts compulsory, the street vendors were selling white T-shirts with a thick black diagonal band. This is the kind of opportunistic anarchy that makes Naples such fun.

Naples can produce virtually anything. The tiny backstreet sweatshops produce much of Italy's *haute couture* – Armani,

Zegna and Valentino all have goods made in Naples. Of course all of these goods can also be bought from street traders at rock bottom prices. Walk down the Corso and you can buy practically any kind of designer accessory from hawkers. Cartier watches, Dupont lighters, Porsche sunglasses, Mont Blanc pens, ersatz one and all. Gold, diamonds and precious stones are also available cheap to the unwary.

The Campania region has been a horticultural centre since Roman times, its warmth and sun producing vast supplies of vegetables and fruit. The Bay of Naples supplies a huge variety of fish and, because of the pollution, questionable shellfish. All of this produce can be bought in the colourful and noisy street markets. Just off the Corso, the main street, there is a fish market. On display are fish, mostly alive in water, and shellfish in buckets that squirt you as you pass. Octopus climb continually out of whatever receptacle they're in, only to be bundled straight back in again by the fish-monger. Solitary mullet eye you gloomily from shallow trays of water. The merchants constantly throw water over their wares and occasionally their customers; the pavements are wet with splashes and overflows.

There are other street markets where you can buy, under the watchful eye of local *carabinieri*, cigarettes clearly marked 'PX stores' or 'duty free'. Since Italy ran, until recently, a state monopoly on tobacco, these are clearly illegal, yet no one seems to mind. A cynic may also suspect that electrical white goods, sold at a third of the normal retail cost, might well be stolen. I once heard a story that some years ago an American warship came to Naples on a courtesy visit, prob-ably from the nearby Nato base in Gaeta. Unwisely, all the sailors were granted shore leave, and the ship was docked in the harbour. For months afterwards the contents of the stripped ship were on sale from hawkers and in the markets. 'Pssst. You wanna buy seegarettes? Wheesky? Radar?'

Naples has that kind of reputation. The gauche, the clumsy

and the inept – which often includes tourists – are fair game. Neapolitans, like all Italians, respect the *furbo*, the smart, and despise the *fesso*, the naïve. People who walk the streets gormlessly with a wallet stuck in their hip pocket can expect no mercy. People who pay the first price asked of them are marked at once as *fesso*. These are people who command no respect, which to a southern Italian male is like losing one's manhood. A man may be poor, live in a hovel, but he must command respect for his ability to navigate the rocky shallows of life.

Part of the obsession with being *furbo* – what the Irish call being a 'cute hoor' – is never being seen to lose face. Being conned is more than bad luck in Italy; it means that you're not as *furbo* as you should be. Publicly making someone look *fesso* is about the worst thing you could do. People have lifelong feuds with others who made them look *fesso*. Seducing a man's wife is bad enough, but making a woman leave her husband is serious. Not only has the seducer put horns on the husband, something many Italian men learn to live with, but the husband is publicly seen not to have been able to satisfy his wife. This is a nearly mortal slur on his manhood.

One of the joys and irritations of village life is that your personal history becomes communal property. Stories are repeated in bars and at tables and become part of the local folklore. Families have their own traditions of stories from previous generations and mine is no exception. My great-uncle Ferdinando is remembered for much, but it is how he was *fregato* with his donkey that is remembered best.

As a child I remember him as an old, wiry man with grey hair and a grey beard sitting at the head of the table, a 2-litre bottle of his own wine on the floor beside him that was not for sharing. Uncle Ferdinando had a donkey. It was a grey donkey with a wall eye and an evil temperament, much given to breaking out and running along the road to the hamlet of San Andrea. The donkey was causing Uncle

Ferdinando a severe loss of face – *brutta figura*; he was teased unmercifully until at last he took action.

Monday is market-day in Atina. The piazza is filled with stalls selling clothes, hardware, food and animals. It was to Atina that Uncle Ferdinando led his donkey early one Monday morning. By modern standards it's a long walk, over Ponte Corno on to what then was the main road to Isernia, through the hamlet of Settignano, on to Ponte Melfa, where the road from Sora joins up, and over the river once more to begin the climb to Atina, some 250 metres up. I know of no witness to the event, but the story goes that Uncle Ferdinando eventually managed to sell his wall-eyed pest to a gypsy horse-dealer. Blessing his luck to be rid of the beast and drinking to its farewell, he came home to tell my aunt of his cleverness in foisting this animal upon a hapless and gullible gypsy.

And yet, as the weeks passed, it seemed that Uncle Ferdinando missed the beast. He began to invent reasons as to why a donkey would be of use around the farm, how only a donkey could use the mule tracks that led up from the farm, through the small highland plain of La Macchia, up to the Maddonna Sarra, high up La Silara, where only charcoal burners and shepherds ventured. Here Uncle Ferdinando went hunting; even in the 1930s game was scarce in Italy from over-shooting, and only in such high, inaccessible places could ptarmigan and partridge be found. A donkey was the only way to get there, he declared. And so, having convinced himself of its necessity, Uncle Ferdinando went once more to Atina to buy a donkey.

As luck would have it, the same gullible fool that had bought the donkey was there. My uncle, like most Italians, enjoyed getting the better of a bargain, and the horse-dealer seemed a perfect foil for him. The man recognized him and smiled broadly, clearly harbouring no grudges over the donkey he had bought some weeks earlier. No, he had no donkeys for sale this week, he had only horses and mules. Uncle Ferdinando was about to go when he saw a brown donkey tethered to the railings behind the stall. This was not for sale, it was the horse-dealer's personal property. Uncle Ferdinando decided that he liked the look of it, and determined to have it. They argued, they fought, they cursed one another for pig-headedness and inability to compromise, and eventually the deal was done. Uncle Ferdinando had the better of the gypsy and bought the donkey, not before parting with a good deal of money.

In the bar on the square Uncle Ferdinando drank his own good health, and once more relished a victory over a gypsy horse-dealer. Their reputation for craftiness was, he decided, a myth – or, if it were true, how much the cleverer had he been for twice getting the better of a gypsy.

Uncle strode home, leading his new donkey, whose coat glistened in the sun, who looked at him with two good eyes and not the blank Cyclopian stare of his last wall-eyed beast. They crossed the river at Ponte Melfa, and by the time they had walked to Settignano it began to rain; gently at first, and then as only the Apennines know how, a deluge of biblical proportions. A clap of thunder, and the donkey took off at full gallop down the road, leaving Uncle Ferdinando cursing and swearing.

He stopped chasing the donkey as gradually a realization dawned on him. If this was the horse-dealer's own donkey, where would it run to, but back to its owner? Uncle toyed with the idea of returning to Atina, but for sure the horse-dealer, the donkey and his money would be gone. And so his joy turned to bitterness and he walked home through the rain cursing his luck and his own gullibility for dealing with a gypsy.

What really rankled was the knowledge that this horse-thief would be laughing with his gypsy pals over his misfortune. Uncle now found himself with no donkey and money lost, too. Wearily he turned off the road at the fountain, and walked past the family chapel to the yard before the house. The stable door was open, and Pepe, who worked on the farm, was standing in the doorway.

'Did you get a donkey?' asked Pepe.

'No,' Uncle replied, telling half the truth.

'You've got one now,' said Pepe, still laughing. 'Come and see.'

Inside the stable stood a piebald donkey, part grey, part brown. Little rivulets of brown rain ran off the donkey's back into a brown puddle on the floor. Uncle rubbed the donkey's coat with his hand: it turned brown. Pepe was laughing uncontrollably.

'You bought your old donkey back again, didn't you?'

'It's got two good eyes. It can't be.'

Closer examination showed nothing more complicated than black paint, straight on to the wall-eyed cornea. Brown stain was still running out of the donkey's soaking coat.

'I couldn't believe it,' said Pepe. 'I heard galloping down on the road, and then this donkey turned into our drive at full gallop, into the yard and straight into his stable. Knew his way home all right.'

At first Uncle Ferdinando consoled himself with the change in the donkey's personality, which seemed more permanent than his colour change. For two days the donkey was quiet, calm and easy to handle. 'That's the gypsies for you,' he said. 'They know how to put manners on these beasts.' But then the effect of the large lump of sausage the donkey had been fed wore off. The savage constipation that this *mortadella* had produced in the donkey eventually passed, and with it the donkey's good nature. I am told that Uncle never again tried to dispose of the donkey, and referred to it from then on as 'my cross'.

The phrases *farsi fregare*, or *una fregatura* – to let yourself be conned, or a con – are always used with a world-weary sadness in the voice, as opposed to '*L'ho fregato bene*' – 'I really got the better of that poor sap' – which is said with a voice full of glee. We were once eating in a small restaurant in Naples, obviously a lunch-time haunt of Neapolitan business-men. I couldn't help overhearing the conversation at the table behind me, where four men were talking about Rome.

'I had to go to Rome last week,' ventured one, 'and I was worried sick about being *fregato*. You really can't trust those Romans.'

'What happened?' enquired another.

'Nothing. I got out OK.'

What amused me about this trivial exchange was that here were men who had mastered the labyrinthine machinations of Naples – a city holding immeasurable perils of *la fregatura* for an entire nation of Italians – worrying about being ripped off in Rome. It seemed absurd, yet we were witnessing one of Italy's recurring neuroses.

If all this gives the impression that Naples is a chaotic donnybrook of noise and bustle, good. It is. But is also a city of great beauty and charm. The restaurants at Santa Lucia on stilts over the sea, the sight of Vesuvio across the Bay, are the stuff memories are made on. Despite the fact that it is a city where a lot of people make a living from the gullibility of others, the only place I did get done was not in Naples, but in a junk shop in Sora. It was more than twenty years ago, but I remember it well. I was rooting through junk, when the owner asked me if I would be interested in something very old. I said that I would be, and he took me into his office.

'These,' he said, 'are two Etruscan statuettes. They're contra-band, you understand, and that's why they're not in the shop, but I could see that you knew what you were looking for, a man with a keen eye . . .' I succumbed. I bought them.

As it happened, we were due in Rome that evening for dinner with an old friend of my father, Professor Pasqualino Rotondi. He headed the Restoration Department in the

Ministry of Fine Arts, and was just the man to appreciate my discovery. We ate dinner *al fresco* in a restaurant in Trastevere and over coffee I handed over my little package silently.

Silently the professor eyed them, and then pronounced: '*La solita patacca*' – 'the usual rubbish'.

Needless to say, they were neither old nor Etruscan. My father, however, was sufficiently enraged, partly I suppose because of the public loss of face, to take the dealer to court. While I was in Ireland we won. I forgot all about it, until in 1990, more than twenty years later, a sergeant of the *carabinieri* came to my house and handed me a packet. Italian justice had finally run its course, and two tiny statuettes came home.

The reputation for *la fregatura* that Naples holds even finds official expression. The last service station before Naples on the A2 motorway from Rome has a notice outside the lavatories in four languages; the English reads, 'Beware of Abusive Traders.' This is not, as it appears, the work of some anonymous member of the Polite Society, but rather the work of a man with a dictionary; it is a transliteration of the Italian word *abusivo*, which today means unlawful, and never, if ever, abusive.

The word *abusivo* is one you hear a lot in Italy. 1 April 1988 was the last day for anyone to regularize with the authorities any building they might possess that did not have the blessing of planning permission – it is the buildings that are *abusivi*, not their owners. The proverbial casual observer could be forgiven for believing that in Italy there is no such thing as planning permission, or that, should such a thing exist, it is clearly available to anyone who wants it for any construction he might desire. All over the landscape there are half-finished concrete skeletons placed as though beauty and sensibility were concepts far removed from Italian culture.

Planning permission in Italy comes from the town hall, not from the province or region. Since the vast majority of Italy's *comuni* are small, with less than 3,000 inhabitants, it stands to reason, at least to a politician, that permission refused is a vote lost. As a result, the biggest sinners in this respect have been small towns and, as usual, southern Italy heads the list. A copy of *Il Messaggero* of 1988 carried some interesting statistics. In the province of Bolzano, formerly the German Bozen, there were only 2,400 buildings that were *abusivi*. Of these, 2,300 owners came forward, paid their fines and regularized their position. In Naples, on the other hand, 10,000 requests had been received to legalize unlawful buildings, a figure that seems large, until you discover that there are entire townships on the outskirts of Naples with no planning permission whatsoever.

In the Comino Valley an estimated 10 per cent or less of the owners of unlawful buildings have paid their fines, which means that 90 per cent live with the possibility of sequestration. They seem to know what I only suspect: the possibility is remote.

The debate in Italy is not how great a fine to levy on the law-breakers, or whether the 'abusive' houses should be pulled down, but rather whether Italy needs the law or not. There already exist constraints on the granting of planning permission by town councils: for example, you need a hectare of land to build a new house; it cannot be within 50 metres of a river. Despite the many constraints, permission is granted for buildings that are clearly in breach of regulations. There is a law which forbids building within a set distance from a cemetery, yet in Gallinaro there is a house which abuts on to the cemetery wall.

The Latin mind is capable of great flexibility. It understands that on the one hand there is a need for order in construction and on the other that a poor man must build a house on the only piece of land he owns, even if it happens to be in a green belt. Just as the Latin mind can perceive these two exigencies, it administers accordingly. Thus the equity that the law in its starkness lacks is supplied by the administrators at local level.

This is the great dilemma of Italian local politics: does the mayor who grants planning permission where clearly it should be denied do it to remedy an injustice, or to get a vote?

Conversations in bars turn on such split hairs. Everyone agrees that there should be some kind of regulation, some sort of plan. But just as everyone agrees that there should be a town dump and no one wants it next to their garden, no one wants a regulation so tight, so all-encompassing, that it might some day affect themselves.

Looking around the Comino Valley, it is hard to see how someone who has built a six-storey block without permission thinks that he won't get found out. The evidence is there for all to see. There is a man in Gallinaro who got permission to build four apartments and who built six, with a large *pizzeria* and shops as well. No one finds this outrageous, but they are annoyed that for all the plumbing in so large an edifice he has not included a septic tank, the sewerage being allowed to flow freely over the road.

The Italian attitude to the law has always been this ambivalent. There is a pervasive respect for countries where laws are perceived to be administered impartially without fear or favour, something that has never been possible in Italy. The laws here are vague, complex and sometimes Draconian: justice is administered erratically. Far from being seen as protection for the individual against the vagaries of authority, it is seen as a weapon of the state to keep its citizens off-balance. No one can be entirely sure what the ramifications of any new law might be. Despite this, the laws can nearly always be evaded or avoided by an astute citizen, secure in the knowledge that, should some infraction of a law take place, the wheels of justice turn so slowly that a conviction can be delayed almost interminably.

About six years ago, just arrived, I was lighting a cigarette in the local bar when a friend said: 'Hope you have that lighter taxed.'

'What?'

'Got the lighter taxed.'

It wasn't a joke. As a measure to protect lighter manufacturers from dumped Japanese disposables, any disposable had to
be taxed. This was done, as many lesser taxes are in Italy, by
buying a special stamp, a *marco da bollo*, from a licensed
tobacconist. An untaxed disposable lighter was subject to
confiscation by the fiscal police. Spectres of dawn raids.
'Come out with your hands up, with all your lighters!' Bar
conversation revolved for weeks on how this law could be
circumvented. The general consensus was that the economics
of the tax made the occasional confiscation the cheaper option.
It was also suggested that the law may not have had the
wholehearted support of the fiscal police, who quite possibly
would feel a little silly demanding to see taxed lighters. The
law also appeared to apply to cigarette lighters in cars, so for
a few weeks most motorists would put the car cigarette
lighter in their pockets while driving. Mention this law today
and you'll get a shifty sort of silence. Like any bad law that is
unenforceable, it has simply died from neglect.

The Italian dislike of taxation has prompted the government
to some extraordinary measures. It was once calculated that if
an individual were to honestly pay every tax to the last lira,
he would find himself paying more than 100 per cent of his
income. The system assumes dishonesty of massive proportions and thus manages to collect something close to the
European average of income tax. Some years ago an attempt
was made to shame taxpayers by publishing in each town hall
the personal tax paid by each taxpayer. Far from shaming
people, it became a matter of pride to stay in the bottom half
of the list – only the *fessi*, the fools, were in the top half. The
list I saw one year was laughable. The top place was taken by
a man who had paid two million lire, about £1,000. This man
is a rich builder, who owns three apartment blocks that I
know of.

There is another quirk in the system of assessing personal liability: it is done by meeting an inspector, arguing the case that you are in penury and then agreeing a figure. It is not unknown for people to have special suits and shirts that are clearly old, but which show signs of meticulous mending about the cuffs and collars, creating an air of respectable poverty. It makes a good base from which to begin negotiations. Being Italy, tax and VAT inspectors will often do a deal which saves the taxpayer money while enriching the civil servant.

The tax-law which has had the most far-reaching effect on behaviour came into effect in 1989. Since then all shop-keepers have been obliged to have a cash register with a double till-roll that prints receipts. Any transaction, however small, must be rung up on the register. It is an offence not to issue a receipt, and an offence not to take one. It must also be carried from the shop by the purchaser for at least 50 metres, for within that distance he can be stopped and required to produce a receipt for the items in his possession. If not, both the seller and the purchaser are liable to a fine of £250.

This Draconian law is certainly effective in dealing with tax evasion and limiting the black economy, but it has produced some insane moments. Over-eager *guardie di finanza* have busted school-children buying sweets with no receipt. A woman was arrested for leaving a hairdresser's shop with no receipt even though the hairdresser was her son and there had been no charge. Unfortunately I feel sure that before long this system will be adopted by other European states, eager to increase revenues and extend their influence.

Italy always appears to travellers as a country of happy-go-lucky people, laughing, shouting and gesticulating, but with little organization or control. On the surface this may be so, but it is far from the truth. There are many agents of the state, all of whom have powers, should they wish to use them, to make the life of a citizen uncomfortable. There are many kinds of uniformed police, each with their own area of influence and power. At the local level there is the *guardia*, or *vigile urbano*. Like all policemen, they are armed. There are traffic police, *carabinieri*, and fiscal police. All of these are much in evidence. Foreign motorists are unlikely to notice – I have never been stopped while driving a foreign-registered car – but in an Italian car you can reasonably expect to be stopped about twice a week, asked to produce your documentation and a thorough check made of the car. If no documents are forthcoming, the car can be impounded. Any fault, such as faulty lights or insufficient tread on the tyres, is subject to an on-the-spot fine. See how far you can drive at night with a tail-light out before you get stopped and fined.

The state is concerned to know the whereabouts of all its citizens. If I were to sell my house in Gallinaro and move to Rome, I would be obliged to officially transfer my residence to Rome, and re-register my car with Roman plates. In this way an out-of-area car is easily spotted, and can be checked at any one of the myriad roadside check-points. You must at all times carry your identity card, to prove who you are to any inquisitive policeman, something I find hard to remember having spent many years in England and Ireland.

Italians, on the other hand, find it hard to understand how a state can have any control over its citizens when there is neither an identity card, nor, until recently, a driving-licence with a photograph. I have suggested that a man who wishes to disguise his identity from the police in Ireland could supply a false name and address, and in Italy could supply a false identity card. The point is that the majority of people are law-abiding and to me it seems unfair that they should be put to some inconvenience simply to make control of the wayward few easier for the police. This is an argument that I have never had accepted in Italy. A similar line of reasoning, against the necessity for a photograph on a driving-licence, meets with a similar response. It occurs to me that a signature ought to be sufficient, since even in Italy a signature is sufficient on the bottom of a cheque, allowing many millions of lire to be paid out.

Perhaps it is simply that Italians are aware of the waywardness of their national character and know that without sufficient checks and balances life could become more unpredictable than it is already. There is a deep vein of insecurity running through Italian life, a racial memory of a history of constant flux. Just as the farmers of the last century struggled to keep their crops from the marauding brigands, today the fear is economic chaos. There were not always thousands of lire to the pound. Massive inflation during and after the last World War wiped out the savings of millions of Italians. Many people who had their money in property lost it all in bombing raids. Earthquakes have also destroyed properties. In 1921 Sora had a massive earthquake, destroying most of the old town. Compensation was eventually paid in 1989, but lira for lira – damage estimated at 2,000 lire in 1921 was paid as 2,000 lire in 1989.

Italy has now had the longest sustained period of prosperity in its history, but the suspicion remains in the minds of all Italians that well-being is just a temporary blip in what is essentially a vale of tears. The chaos of the past has left indelible marks on the psyche; Italians have a powerful urge to *sistemare*, a word that can be rendered in English as 'to bring order into chaos'. But the word has wider usage in Italian. Italians are keen to *sistemarsi*, to get themselves into a position of comfort and power, where the vagaries of fortune cannot find them. Southern Italians used to believe that a job in the civil service would fit the bill, but government cutbacks have made even this cushy number as shaky as any other. If an Italian tells you that he wants to *sistemare* his house, he doesn't mean tidy it up. He means put it right, fix the leaks, add a bathroom, put in a septic tank. There is a constant push to improve, to *sistemare*.

Currently Naples is the basket-case of Italy. Water supplies are irregular, milk vans have armed escorts, many of its politicians are under arrest or investigation. The Camorra, Naples' home-grown version of the Mafia, still has tentacles throughout the city and its administration.

A friend told me that Italy's only long-term hope was to follow the Neapolitan example. Neapolitans have never believed in the mirage of stability – they know that all is flux. They have maintained their flexibility and can cope almost instantaneously with anything fortune may throw at them. Perhaps the adaptability of the Neapolitans is only the sharper edge of one of the great strengths of the Italian nation.

# 7

## *Racial Memories*

The Comino Valley takes its name from the battle of Cominium, described by Livy in Book X of his history of Rome. The Romans had begun their push southward and found themselves in conflict with the Samnites, whose territory included the valley. The Romans initially suffered one of their most humiliating defeats at the hands of the Samnites at the Caudine Forks and were forced to sign a peace treaty. For thirty years it rankled, until, under the pretext that the consuls had no right to sign the peace treaty, the Romans once more went to war with the Samnites, and this time won, establishing hegemony over most of southern Italy. The battle of Cominium was one of the first defeats for the Samnites. Livy puts it at twelve leagues from Atina, but since this is the only geographical information he gives, the site of Cominium itself is not clear. Accepted wisdom puts the site at Vicalvi, the small promontory which dominates the western end of the valley.

The valley is flooded with history, its marks are at every turn. Farmers consistently plough up pottery shards and sometimes artefacts of bronze, iron, silver or gold. Three Norman castles are now churches, a Roman bridge still stands over the Melfa. Surrounding Atina are the pre-Roman polygonal walls. The history of these walls is interesting. Their origin is unclear; some archaeologists believe them to be Pelasgian, dating them to between 2500 and

2000 BC. Others believe them to be Mycenaean Greek, dating them to between 1500 and 1000 BC. These peoples would have come by sea to Cassino, which at that time was at the head of a long and deep fjord. Roughly 4 kilometres of wall remain out of an estimated 8-kilometre perimeter. Three perimeter walls can be traced, the largest of them enclosing 110 hectares. Clearly, long before Roman times Atina was a city of some importance, since the areas enclosed by other city walls was much smaller – Mykonos, the largest city of antiquity, was 30 hectares, Athens 25 and Troy only 10.

There is a sense of continuous human presence, unbroken through the dim recesses of history. At Posta Fibreno, at the western end of the valley, an enormous spring bursts out from under the Apennines, clear and very cold, which forms a lake before flowing westwards as the River Fibreno to join the Liri. This is a stunningly beautiful place, about which Marcus Tullius Cicero wrote in *De Legibus*:

> We walk
> Between the high poplars
> Along the banks
> Shimmering emerald, opaque.
> We have arrived at the island.
> There is nothing
> More beautiful than this:
> Here it is
> That the Fibreno opens
> Like a bird's beak.
> Here is my real home
> And my brother's too.
> From here we spring
> From ancient stock;
> Here all that we call holy,
> Here our relations,

Here so many memories
Of our ancestors.

What struck me so strongly was that Cicero thought this place full of ancient memories, and he of ancient stock. How much more so, 2,000 years later. How hard to see the struggle of a human lifetime as much more than a comma in the valley's long record of history.

I have always had an interest in Cicero. For years I fondly imagined myself to be descended from him. His name was Marcus Tullius and he was born in Arpino, which adjoins Casalattico. Local legend has it that Casalattico takes its name from Casalis Attici, the home of Pomponius Atticus, Cicero's friend and publisher. The inference is that Cicero must have had contact with the Comino Valley and may even have had family there, since they were wool merchants by trade. Tullio is common enough in Italy as a Christian name, but rare as a surname; to the best of my knowledge it is found almost exclusively in Gallinaro. All this fanned my belief that he was an ancestor, until I discovered that he manumitted about 300 slaves, who by way of thanks for their freedom took Tullius as their surname. This makes the odds on descent from Cicero pretty thin and I have abandoned it as a theory – instead I now claim descent from Servius Tullius, sixth king of Rome. Cicero, incidentally, means chick-pea, and referred to a wart on his nose. Sad that he should be known throughout history by the name of a facial blemish.

Roman names are not used in Italy with the final '-us' ending as in English but rather with the later Latin vulgate 'o'. So the man known as Livy to generations of schoolboys in the English-speaking world is called Tito Livio in Italy; Cicero is Marco Tullio Cicerone; Ovid is Ovidio; Marius is Caio Mario. Knowing them by their Italian names makes them somehow less remote and more immediate.

Because the valley has been continually inhabited for thousands of years this historical continuum finds echoes in almost all strands of daily life. In my local dialect there are words not found in modern Italian, phonetically transliterated roughly as *poscra*, *mo*, *yic*, which are nearly pure Latin for 'the day after tomorrow', 'now', and 'here'. As television permeates Italian life, so local dialects are declining, but there is one way in which the dialects still thrive. *Feste* are as important to Italians as wine and sun, and at every *festa* in my valley there is always a performance in dialect of a ribald sketch. The cast varies little: an old peasant farmer, a spirited daughter, a foolish son, a crafty old woman – all descended in unbroken line from the Atellan farces, originally performed in Oscan (the language of an early Italic people), which degenerated in Roman times to crude mime, but survived in the provinces to become the vulgar belly-laughs of today.

The word 'dialect' can cause confusion. In the UK and Ireland it conjures up the rolling consonants of the rural counties, where all that really changes is the accent and perhaps an odd word or two peculiar to the region. In Italy a dialect is really a language, often with its own written tradition and more often than not very different from Italian. Once again the reasons for this are historical: from the break-up of the Roman Empire until the last century, Italy was a loose agglomeration of city states, each with its own traditions and culture. Obviously, states that bordered one another, such as Siena and Florence, had virtually identical languages, whereas if a Neapolitan were to speak in Neapolitan to a Milanese, the latter would understand virtually nothing of the conversation. What we know today as Italian is the language of Tuscany, the language of the great writers of the Italian Golden Age: Boccaccio, Dante and Petrarch. This was the language used by educated men from all parts of the Italic peninsula to talk to one another, much as Latin once was.

What this means is that for many Italians, Italian is their second language. Most people speak their own patois most of the time, saving Italian for conversations with strangers. My friend the poet Gerardo Vacana, in common with many erudite men, delights in speaking Gallinarese rather than Italian. He says he finds it richer in similes. This is true, but in my experience the similes are nearly all agricultural. Until recently I laboured under the misapprehension that I could enrich my Italian simply by speaking to Italians. I have belatedly learnt that this is not a good idea. Oddly most Italians do not speak good Italian. It is rare to find someone with enough interest or pride to really study it and speak it as it should be spoken. When it is well spoken, it is a delight to listen to.

The movement towards a common language encompassing all of Italy has been so successful, thanks to radio and television, that in late 1991 the Italian government felt confident enough to reverse the Italicization policy of Mussolini and pass a new law admitting twenty-two new official languages. These range from Albanian, Croatian, Slovene, Greek, German and French to the regional dialects from Italy's extremities. Greek, by the way, is still spoken in parts of southern Italy that were, prior to the hegemony of Rome, part of greater Greece nearly 2,500 years ago. The immediate effect of this new law will be to allow towns and street names to revert to their original names, should their inhabitants wish them to do so.

The close link to a 2,500-year-old tradition may seem unusual at this distance from the Mediterranean, but in Italy it results in a casual and sometimes cavalier attitude to antiquity. Italian laws are strict: wherever there is evidence of archaeological interest, the Ministry of Fine Arts steps in and blocks any kind of interference with the site. This is fine, except that the whole Italian peninsula is of archaeological interest. So, for modern man to go about his business, these laws are frequently ignored or evaded. I know of a man who bought a site for a holiday villa near Terracina, where the emperor Tiberius liked to while away the summer. When the foundations were sunk, they revealed the site of a Roman villa. Mosaics and amphorae were discovered. These were immediately destroyed, to ensure that the building would continue. The fact is that the Ministry of Fine Arts has enough sites to keep it occupied for the next few centuries at current rates of excavation, so what in some countries would be seen as wanton destruction of priceless artefacts becomes in Italy a sort of cull.

Archaeological treasures are also the cause of Rome's lack of an extensive underground railway. Since Mussolini's day every attempt to expand the system has ground to a standstill within a few metres, since, no matter in what direction they dig, some new archaeological wonder is discovered. As far as I know, there have been many starts, but the system remains with only one more line than Mussolini left it with.

The most perfect example I can think of to demonstrate the layering of history on the landscape is in Pompei. The city is divided along its east–west axis by the Cardus Maximus, the main street. About half-way along its length it bounds the unexcavated quarter. To get a better view of the city, I climbed up to the first floor of a building and found behind and 5 metres below me sprawled a city, while in front of me was an agrarian landscape of fields, maize and vines covering the as yet unexposed part of Pompei. It was easy to see how it was lost for so long. The fields looked no different from millions of others and yet below them was a city. Life continues on the surface as it had on the old.

We visit Pompei most years and now know it quite well. The last occasion brought out some bad behaviour in me. While my wife was painting in the Triangular Forum I sat idly on the steps of the Temple of Hercules, bored. Mindless fiddling led me to discover that the ring-pulls which littered the ground were sharp enough to cut into the stone steps. While Susie painted I cut stone. Eventually I had it – *Me transmitte sursum caledoni* – a little Latin graffito to confound anyone able to make out 'Beam me up, Scottie'. I was delighted with this, and when we got back to Gallinaro I told Silvano how clever I'd been. As the curator of antiquities in Cassino, he was outraged. 'You're a vandal That's a disgraceful thing to do. *Maleducato.*' I'm still proud of my riposte. 'Since I came here from the north, at least I'm in the mainstream tradition of vandals arriving to deface and destroy.'

A walk along the streets of Pompei is an eye-opener: there are bars, laundries, bakeries and hotels. The bigger houses have extensive gardens, central heating and a large number of rooms, some adapted for summer living and some for winter. There is an air of civilized prosperity about the place that shook my belief in the linear advance of civilization from the Stone Age to today. A look at a reconstruction of a medieval town shows how far things can slide in a thousand years.

I can remember being taught that the tiny suits of armour in the Tower of London show clearly man's inexorable rise from the puny specimens of the Middle Ages to today's strutting six-footers. Imagine my surprise, then to find that the Roman army's great reformer, Caius Marius, dropped the height qualification for legionaries to 5 foot 10 inches; up to the second century BC they had been taller. A surprise, too, to read that the Romans were apprehensive when they first encountered the Celts living in the Po Valley. The Romans were alarmed at the size of the Celtic warriors – 6 foot plus, presumably, and, since the Celts went to war with their hair white-washed to stand upright like a horse's mane, adding to their height, and often fought stark naked but for a little woad, Roman consternation is understandable.

I'm sure that Cicero, that champion of the Roman Republic, would have been appalled to learn that the lessons of history were lost on his successors. Rome, which abolished its monarchy in favour of a republic, had learnt early that stability comes with franchise, not through dictatorship, yet this didn't stop Octavian from establishing himself as emperor and abolishing the republic.

Later the emperor Caracalla, who inherited an empire where only Roman citizens paid tax, had the great idea of making everyone in the empire a citizen. Now he could, and did, tax everyone. Money flowed in and Rome, which he found in brick, was rebuilt with marble. The great baths that bear his name were a product of this new cash inflow. Of course things happened slightly slower then, but within fifty years the complaints began: 'How odd it is to see a Roman face these days in the Forum; nowadays one sees only Numidians, Dacians, Celts, Germans and Mauretanians.' Ah, the cycles of history. Two millennia later the British Empire had the same bright idea – make them all British citizens. And then, before long, those same citizens were seeking residence at the heart of the empire.

Looking back through history, it is clear that the argument between the advocates of empire and the advocates of local, ethnic independence has never been resolved. Before the rise of Rome Italy was divided into areas which were clearly defined, but for minor border skirmishes. In the north-east there were the Ligurians, in the Po Valley the Celts, to the south the Etruscans, south of them the Latins, then the Samnites, with the Greeks occupying the far south and Sicily. Between these major blocs, there were minor states such as the Osci, the Volsci and the Sabines. From 1500 BC to 500 BC there was some stability. However, the later dominion of Rome over most of the Mediterranean basin brought much greater prosperity, not least because piracy on the sea was virtually ended, there were no borders, and a common currency made trade easier and more profitable. Empire seemed the way forward.

From the break-up of the Roman Empire until the Middle Ages individual states traded and fought. And then, in the sixteenth century, the imperialist drive began again. The British Empire was in the ascendant. Since its demise we have seen the rise of the American Empire, and the disintegration of the Russian. The former Soviet states are currently debating among themselves what the Italians argued about at the time of Dante: empire or loose confederation.

By the Middle Ages Italy had evolved into a patchwork of city-states, each with its own history of trade and war, of rights won and liberty defended. Some of these states were rich and powerful: Milan, Venice, Genoa and Florence. Others were less strong, but maintained their integrity by the politics of *The Prince* and the arm of a powerful friend. A look at a map will show that these mighty states, whose trade routes stretched from the Hanseatic Baltic states to the Orient, all lie to the north of Rome. These city-states, although headed by a prince or a duke, had governments that shared power between the head of state and other citizens such as nobles and merchants. They were by no means universally enfranchised democracies, but the citizenry had a voice in the running of the state and the pursuit of their common weal.

The great debate among these states in medieval Italy was between the Guelphs and the Ghibellines. To simplify the complexities of this period, the Guelphs supported the rights of the city-states to a separate existence, while the Ghibellines were supporters of empire – that is, of a super-state combining all the city-states, with the supposed benefits of greater stability and trade. Drawing on the history of the Hellenistic city-states 2,000 years before, the Ghibellines pointed out that had Athens, Sparta, Macedon and the smaller states become one pan-Hellenic state, undoubtedly their history of subsequent subjugation would have been different. The parallels with the Italic states were irresistible – there was a common language, a common history and culture. It made sense to unite for the greater good. In the end the city-states retained their individual identities and flourished. It is no accident that the great names of the Italian *rinascimento* were from the north. There the fire that drives a man to fulfil his personal destiny was not repressed and dampened by feudal authority. A citizen could consider himself an equal amongst equals – in theory at least – and not subject to the whims and caprices of a king.

These are, of course, gross generalizations, but not misleading ones; Dante, Mantegna, Michelangelo, da Vinci, Galileo and Bernini, to pick a few at random, were all from city-states. It cannot be unfair to suggest that it is the way of ordering society that produces these results rather than random chance. The suffocating repression that allowed the trial and conviction of Galileo Galilei had far-reaching effects upon Italian cultural life. The fire of science and learning that had burned with such intellectual brilliance ran from the dousing. When inquiring minds could no longer speak in universities for fear of censure, they took the only course open and fled to the Low Countries. Italy's pre-eminence in art and science waned. Anything of importance was now conceived far from Italy; the Protestant countries became the blast furnace for the displaced fire.

From such generalizations I would conclude that man functions at his best when unchained. His fulfilment becomes the wealth of the state. The south of Italy was ever chronically poor and yet was, on the whole, more ordered. Observation of this paradox prompted Adam Smith to remark that individual wealth, despite itself and without intending to be so, is of benefit to society as a whole. The history of the north juxtaposed with that of the south would seem to confirm this.

It would be obtuse not to recognize that to work a flat alluvial plain is easier and more profitable than to terrace a mountainside. Clearly, geography was on the side of the Po Valley farmers, whose produce was the basis of the later wealth of the northern states. Curiously, to this day the mainstay of southern Italy's economy is agriculture, even though the land is mountainous, top-soil is sparse and water scarce. Surely it is here that manufacturing industry should be sited. So obvious a point as this was spotted even by the government, who set up the Cassa del Mezzogiorno, a kind of industrial development authority, whose function was to place industry in the south. It has for the most part been an expensive failure. The southern workers took days off to tend their land, livestock or harvest, disrupting assembly lines without a thought. Creation of wealth does not form part of the cultural values of the south; centuries of feudalism are deeply engrained. It is still the north that makes most of the money that runs the Italian state – its people still have the drive that history has bequeathed.

The perceived disparity of wealth generated by the north and the south, despite government attempts to play it down, has caused a new political force to emerge – the northern Lombard League. It aims to divide Italy into two, although the exact point of demarcation is not quite clear. Historically, the divide would be to the north of Rome, creating the northern super-state beloved of the Ghibellines, while the feudal south would be left to its own devices. The League has ample ammunition: the Cassa del Mezzogiorno itself has been cynically exploited, enriching a few, but leaving a legacy of empty factories, job-promises never fulfilled and industrial machinery paid for but never materializing. Southern financial scandals are legion, adding grist to the Lombard League's mill.

Garibaldi's greatest triumph, persuading the self-determining states to believe in the power of unity, creating a unified country that could hold its head high among the nations of Europe, resulted in the state we now call Italy. It is a young country; at the age of eight I met an old man who had lived in the Papal States as a boy. The links to the past are far from remote. Unification was a creature of its time: the Germans were united as a nation, a new world order was looming with the coming century's end. It's tempting to draw parallels with this *fin de siècle*.

The difference appears to be that we have now reached the other end of the pendulum's swing. Separatism is on the march again, people are wondering if a centralized monolith of a government is the best arrangement for protecting the rights of individual citizens. The debate continues apace in the Balkans.

Vestiges of the culture of the northern city-states have been incorporated into modern Italy with its four levels of government – national, regional, provincial and local. What is not often recognized outside of Italy is the amount of power wielded by the *comuni*. It is possible to live one's life having recourse only to the town hall for matters concerning the state. Here one applies for planning permission, licences to trade, birth and death certificates, residency, nationality and for the plethora of forms that a citizen is obliged by the state to fill in. As a result of this devolution of power, local preoccupations, prejudices and interests survive and co-exist with those of the central authority, and for most Italians what matters is government in the town hall, not Rome.

Throughout the debate leading up to the 1992 general election in the United Kingdom there were endless references in the press to proportional representation and to how badly it worked in Italy. It was pointed out that the Italian system produced governments of multi-party alliances — coalitions cobbled together that were the antithesis of stable government. This misses the point of the Italian system entirely. Where government really matters, in the town hall, the largest party gets twelve council seats, the opposition three, ensuring stable, single-party government. To the vast majority of Italians going about their daily business, the government in Rome is an irrelevance. This is why more energy is expended on local politics than on national, and why no one in Italy cares very much about the merry-go-round of alliances and coalitions in Rome.

Unlike the British system of local government, where what powers remain are being constantly eroded by the centralized state, Italian *comuni* are well funded and largely autonomous. Whereas in Britain no one bothers to vote at local elections, in Italy they are the most fiercely contended, with a turnout of above 80 per cent most of the time. More machiavellian plots are hatched to elect a town mayor in Italy than a prime minister in another European country.

It is possible that so diverse a country as Italy would not have survived as an entity without this devolution of power to the *comuni*.

# 8

# *Bribesville*

Politics in small villages is, as I have said before, serious business. It affects the pocket. I have little knowledge of regional or national politicking, but close to home, at local level, I have seen it at work.

To put it into some kind of perspective, in Italy every town that has the designation of *comune* has an elected council. Whether a town is a *comune* or not has more to do with history than its size. It's a little like the 1855 classification of Bordeaux *grands crus*: in theory there is re-classification, but in practice precious little. I have been told that there are *comuni* of less than 200 people near the French border, each with their elected town council, whereas many new towns with many thousands of inhabitants are administered by another town which traditionally governed the area. Once upon a time these tiny *comuni* were large enough to merit their classification. Today, even though their population has dropped, they retain their title and rights.

Being a *comune* gives a town advantages: it becomes responsible for its own administration. Large sums of money come from central government for local services, such as roads, schools, sewerage, water supply, rubbish disposal and local policing. These funds, which are considerable, are managed by the elected representatives. In some cases, such as after the 1984 earthquake which hit the Comino Valley at 7.4 on the Richter scale, the funds allocated for rebuilding are enormous

– Gallinaro alone received over £7 million. Being in a position to affect how this money is spent is clearly important.

Let us take a typical, but fictional, town in the valley, which we will call the *comune* of Comino, and look at the mathematics of an election there. The fictional Comino has an official population of 1,000, of which some 700 are voters. A large number of these voters will not actually live in the village; they will live elsewhere, but are kept on the register because funds are allocated from Rome on a per capita basis. I have no figures for individual towns, but officially the Comino Valley has 26,300 inhabitants, whereas the USL, the local health authority, has 18,666 individuals on its books. Since this is the number of people entitled to free medical assistance, you can be sure it represents all living souls in the valley. Bearing this in mind, let's be generous and say there are 650 voters. Of these, past experience tells us, only some 500 will bother to vote. Now we can see at once that what we need for an absolute majority in an election is 251 votes, although if more than two parties present themselves, we could manage with less.

The system at local level works on lists – the Socialists will present a list of councillors to the electorate, as will the Christian Democrats, the Republicans and the ex-Communists. The list of candidates of a given persuasion can be voted for *en masse*, or individually in order of preference using a system of proportional representation.

Suppose I am a Socialist, and I head the Socialist list for election. I need 251 votes, and I have eleven others on my list. If each candidate can bring twenty-one votes, I'm a winner. It is important therefore that I pick as candidates for my list people who are either popular, or have large families. What I don't need is two people from the same family, unless I really can't help it. They would only be bringing the same votes. Ideally my list will include candidates from the different parts of the town, again ensuring votes are not duplicated. Administrative ability is obviously not as important as the ability to bring a block of family votes. Therefore I pick my list from all the major families in the village. This suits my purposes and also that of the families, since they will now have a representative on the town council should my list be elected.

After the election, the winning party gets all twelve candidates on its list elected to the council; the mayor, the vice-mayor and three *assessori*, or administrative officers, are then selected from these councillors. The party with the second largest vote becomes the official opposition, with the three members of their list who topped their poll elected as councillors. This puts the winning party in a strong position, since their four-to-one majority is built into the system.

You might think that this sort of majority would be plenty for anyone to govern effectively, but some valley politicians don't see it that way. In the fictional Comino it has been known for the ruling party to set up its own opposing list at the election – a few trusted friends pretending to be an opposing party when in reality they are not. If they succeed in getting elected, as they did twice, then the mayor controls not only his own list of councillors, but also the three on the fake opposition. In this way there can be no tales out of school, since all the councillors are equally implicated. Even if the fake opposition does not get elected, it still serves the very useful purpose of splitting the real opposition's vote. What makes this all such fun is that the huge numbers of political parties that Italy is famous for are probably just manifestations of the same few.

On the face of it, this electoral system seems straightforward enough, but the fact that a proportional system is used means that a fair amount of horse-trading during the elections can be undertaken. Suppose it suited my purposes better to have the ex-Communists as official opposition to my own

Socialists; I could instruct some of my most trusted supporters to allocate some of their voting preferences to selected ex-Communists. This takes no votes away from my party, but gives perhaps crucial transfer votes to the individuals that I want to help on to the town council. The cost of this help can be agreed beforehand – perhaps support for a municipal project that would benefit from no opposition. This sort of bartering is not unique to Italy; any country can boast of similar dealings. Where Italy begins to differ from the rest is in the immediacy of the relationship between the electors and the elected.

Because the Italian system of self-help through family networks is so well established, a town councillor who is elected by a block family vote will owe his primary allegiance to those who elected him. The idea that a councillor is elected for the communal good – for all the citizens, irrespective of whether or not they voted for him – is not a prevalent one. Sometimes to the untrained eye the administration appears to be unbiased and generous to its opponents. It is unlikely to be quite as it appears; either the opposition is one only in name and is in fact one of us, or it is a genuine opposition whom we wish to court. A careful administration can go on increasing its votes after each election by doing overt favours for members of opposing parties. This works in part by incurring gratitude, but also by leaving in the minds of opponents' supporters a suggestion of collusion, thus weakening their position.

As a mayor's wealth and patronage increases over the years, so does his power. If it is clear that a mayor has at least another ten years in office, then obviously as a citizen my best strategy is to support him overtly to ensure that whatever favours I may need from the administration will be given. A mayor's power increases exponentially with his length of tenure, since when he is well ensconced it makes little sense to be a lone opponent. Little by little opponents dwindle and the mayor's political party grows in number. Italian political parties are not based at grass-roots level on ideology, but are tribal – an extension of the family self-help group. Allegiances are based on self-interest, and even the ex-Communists, who once held the moral high-ground, are now seen as no different from anyone else.

The voters must also adapt their voting strategy to their conditions. Town administrations tend to change after a long-serving mayor, who has been in office for twenty to thirty years, retires or dies. This is a major upset, since alliances and allegiances have to be forged anew. In Italy it is vital to be on the winning side, or at the very least not to be the vociferous spokesman for the losing side. The floating voter is the norm. Even paid-up members of a political party think nothing of cancelling their membership and joining another party should a change of administration demand it. The important thing is to be a friend of the administration, or a respected opponent who needs occasional appeasement.

These are not petty considerations. It is in the gift of the administration to make people very rich indeed, even while staying within the law. Like most of the towns in the valley, the fictional Comino gets its funds from the central coffers, based on its size of approximately 1,000 people. The first part of the funds allocated for the rebuilding after the earthquake of 1984 was just over £2 million. By law each *comune* must appoint an engineer to oversee the work on all the buildings that were affected. His fee, as set out in the legislation, is 20 per cent of the monies spent on rebuilding. So, for the couple of years during which rebuilding takes place, £400,000 is available to the man the administration chooses to appoint. Comino has two resident engineers, one who belongs to the ruling party, the other who heads the opposition. No prizes for guessing who gets the plum.

The earthquake was in many ways the saviour of the valley. Although strong, it was short. Many houses were severely damaged, but none collapsed and no one was seriously injured. The state funds allocated were huge, bearing in mind the size of the towns. It worked out at approximately £25,000 per affected house. For a valley of some 25,000 inhabitants, this represents a major injection of cash and work.

People with long memories recall earthquakes in Sicily that happened twenty years or more ago where the victims are still living in caravans. Why the Comino Valley should have had such generous and prompt help is a matter for conjecture, but our proximity to Rome, the centre of disbursement of funds, must be in part responsible. The rationale behind the state's funding of the rebuilding programme is that all houses are part of the state's patrimony and therefore eligible for aid. Carried to extremes, this line of reasoning results in the rebuilding of mountain villages in the Abruzzi which are no longer inhabited.

A second tranche is due from central funds for the repair of houses that were less affected, and will bring further prosperity. It will also bring further dishonesty to our fictional town. There is dishonesty in the claims that are made by the citizens for repairs, just as there is on the part of the administrators, the builders and the overseers. There are people in the town of Comino who have had cattle barns rebuilt as houses, who have had new rooms built on their houses, who owned empty, dilapidated houses that are now new and rentable. All this courtesy of the state. As no one is unsullied, no one casts the first stone.

Italy is currently undergoing the trauma of seeing its national dirty linen paraded in public. Since the huge bribery scandal centred on Milan and the Mafia's assassinations of Judges Falcone and Borsellino in Sicily, the public has suddenly woken up to the extent of the corruption in public life. The papers have christened it *tangentopoli*, or bribesville. The shock to the national psyche is that the administrations of the north, previously held up as the antithesis of the corrupt southern ones, seem to have their snouts in the same trough.

Italians now recognize that there is nowhere to hide. The corruption is pandemic and is at every level. The choice is a stark one – either continue to live with a system of backhanders and favours on the nod, or make an attempt to reorganize the system. The second option would, in my opinion, have a slim to zero chance of coming into being. Most rational Italians that I speak to are full of admiration for the civic administrations of Germany and Great Britain, which they perceive as treating all citizens equally before the law. It is an ideal to which they feel Italy should aspire. They are also aware that it is unlikely to work in Italy. The established system of families and favours is too ingrained. Besides, at a fundamental level there is self-interest involved.

All the citizens of Comino are aware that, although in theory the law forbids many things, the town hall will almost invariably turn a blind eye to even the most blatant abuses in return for a vote. In effect there is an unspoken conspiracy where everyone benefits from abuses of the system. Only the most naïve fail to take advantage. To put it another way, the current system of institutionalized corruption benefits more people than it harms, so it is unlikely to change. A cynic might also observe that the very people who are in the position of being able to effect a change – the politicians – are the ones who most benefit from the present arrangement.

At the simplest level the corruption begins with 'recommendations'. If my son has recently graduated and is looking for a job, I will recommend him to someone who owes me a favour, or who may be hoping for one from me. This has been the way things work for as long as anyone can remember and the result is that many jobs are filled by people eminently unsuitable for the task. I know of three teachers of English who could not speak the language to save their lives, yet have gainful employment teaching the language to children.

Conversely, I know a schoolmistress who speaks English perfectly, but who has had an immense struggle to find work.

Public appointments are ostensibly filled in Italy by *concorsi*, public examinations. These examinations are both written and oral, and the winner is awarded the job on offer. Before any *concorso* takes place, the names of the members of the examining board are made public, thus ensuring that anyone with the right connections can contact the examiners and recommend their preferred candidate. This works, because, although written work may be subject to later public scrutiny, the performance of the candidate in the oral examination is written on the wind. All that is left are the recollections of the examining board, and so their final selection, based on written and oral submissions, is impossible to dispute.

An even easier way to ensure that the correct candidate gets a given job is to make the job available only when the preferred candidate is free to take it. Many positions are left vacant for a year or two simply to ensure the job goes to a friend. There appears to be no sense that this is unethical; it is seen as the right way to behave to help a friend. Just as an employment agency might take the equivalent of the first month's salary for its fees, a present of a similar amount of cash to the person who arranges a job is normal. They are simply doing unofficially what an agency does officially, so the payment has its own rationale. It follows that a civil servant working in, say, the Ministry of Education has the opportunity to find jobs for a great many teachers, so his earning potential is considerable.

The Italian attitude to a job is that the power of the position should be realized and exploited to the last iota. It is not hard to imagine where the temptations lie for the civil servant who heads the committee that sets the price of milk for Rome and its millions of inhabitants. Would this man be courted by the dairies? As the Romans used to say, '*Cacatne ursus in silvis?*'

Seeking out the power in any position is second nature to Italians; perhaps this is why they make such good bridge players. A fine example of this phenomenon has been uncovered recently. Professor Duilio Poggiolini, head of the Health Ministry's pharmaceuticals division, now in prison, became very rich by allowing the price of pharmaceuticals to rocket, and possibly allowing the sale of suspect ones as well. His wealth is phenomenal. So far the investigators have found a safe in his house containing 6,000 gold guineas, twenty large diamonds, ten silver ingots, hundreds of gold coins and a hundred gold ingots, eight of which weighed a kilo. Magistrates have also found a Swiss bank account with 13 million Swiss francs, twenty other Swiss accounts whose details are still unknown, two Italian accounts holding 75 billion lire – about £31 million. Lastly there are the paintings, sixty of them, including Picassos, Modiglianis and Dalis. Interestingly, the professor was a member of the infamous P2 Masonic lodge.

Traditionally, one of the differences between northern and southern Italians is their attitude to employment by the state. Although the civil service offered security of tenure, a title and a pension, it didn't pay well. Italians from the north, with its developed economy, did not apply, but went for jobs where the money was good. It is still true that the vast majority of civil servants in Italy are from the south. As prosperity has come to Italy, so the money flowing through the hands of the civil servants has grown exponentially. The European Community has added to the administrative burden of handling so much money. Suddenly minor civil servants have within their grasp the chance of riches. Dispensing funds from, for example, the EC's Regional Fund becomes a plum job. Each application that passes the desk is an opportunity for enrichment. This is the reason why so little of the money that is allocated for a given task ever reaches its destination. All along the route there are people taking their *tangente*, their slice of the cake.

Tracking down lost or misplaced funds in Italy is a sequestrator's nightmare. Very rarely is anything recovered and even more rarely is a culprit found. Even when officials are caught *in flagrante delicto*, taped and filmed taking bribes, nothing much happens. Trials can be postponed almost indefinitely, evidence gets misplaced, statutes of limitations come into effect, the public forgets. Because all this is known to prosecution and defence alike, there is rarely any vigour in the prosecution; it's like stirring porridge with a rubber spoon – much effort is expended but little is accomplished. Sooner or later the media circus moves on to a new scandal, new revelations, and new Draconian laws are passed to ensure nothing like this ever happens again. As far as I can see no one has yet lost faith in the law. It must be some racial memory from Roman times, but there is an almost naïve belief that passing a law banning a particular malpractice is somehow the same thing as eradicating the crime itself. Passing a new law is the knee-jerk reaction of government to any crisis and, up to now, it seems to have kept the public happy. Adding a new law to the Civil Code becomes a substitute for action.

A lot of news in Italy makes more sense if simple economics are borne in mind. If a builder gets a contract to build an apartment block after putting in his tender, there is not a lot of room for manoeuvre. All of what he has contracted to do is on view. He could skimp on the quality of the finishes, use a little less cement than he should (apartment blocks have collapsed in Rome from over-eager users of this technique) but basically the builder will be obliged to produce a building much as the one envisaged in the plans. A road presents a different set of circumstances. No one is going to check the depth of the foundations or the final layer of tarmacadam for the length of the road. Anyway, the man whose job it is to oversee that all the materials specified are used will sign any declaration in return for his *tangente*. Unlike a building, a shoddy road means only that three years from now the contract for repair will be up for tender, whereas falling buildings tend to precipitate inquiries and awkward questions, especially if people are dead. So roads make money better than houses. With this firmly in mind, the fact that the roads around Irpinia have been repaired to motorway standard, while the people remain in caravans, begins to make sense. Seemingly mindless or random decisions by officials are very rarely that. It is but simple economics at work.

Roads in Italy serve many purposes. They are a physical manifestation of the Italian urge to *sistemare* all around them. Roads open up areas of countryside to machinery, allowing more land to come into cultivation or forestry available for logging. They are also a means of making a lot of people a lot of money. If a *comune* has not had the good fortune to have had an earthquake, it can obtain significant money from the state for building roads. Obviously any request for financing a road must be accompanied by some sort of reason for needing it. Much thought goes into finding reasons for roads.

The fictional *comune* of Comino includes land on the lower slopes of the Apennines which has been for centuries the preserve of shepherds and, once upon a time, charcoal burners. It is accessible only by mule track and has little value. Suppose I am mayor and I own acres of this wilderness; how fine it would be to have a road going to or through it. Not only would the land be easily accessible, it would be available for building houses, multiplying its value by a factor of ten or twenty. All that is needed is to satisfy the state that the road is necessary and the funds will arrive. It is worth considering what 'satisfying the state' actually means. Clearly, the state must at some point be embodied in an individual whose signature will make it all possible – and who may be responsive to a deal that will benefit all parties.

A corollary to this is that if I, as mayor, have plans for the development of an area of the *comune*, I could set about

buying land there and then, once it is mine, start the development. These simple truths explain much of the landscape:
why housing developments appear in unlikely and curious
places, and why roads lead to the top of a mountain and stop,
not connecting with other roads.

The pattern of behaviour of local administrations is
strangely constant. When a new administration takes over a
town, its first five years of tenure sees a huge output of work.
All kinds of civic projects that somehow never got done are
completed, a sense of urgency and competence abounds.
Projects that have a high visibility – like replacing public
benches, street lights, paving-stones in the piazza, or a new
surface on the main thoroughfare – are all completed with
speed and efficiency. The evidence of a new broom is there
for all to see. The administration establishes itself in the minds
of the electorate as a very different beast from the one it has
supplanted. Meanwhile the administration begins to find its
feet in the netherworld of provincial and regional distribution
of funds. It begins to establish contacts with the building
firms that will be its partners in all civic projects – it begins to
find its allies.

Its next term of office sees less projects of obvious benefit
to the community as a whole, and more that have dubious
value. Slowly the administration, like the pigs in *Animal
Farm*, comes to resemble what it replaced. By the third and
fourth term the *comune* will have become the personal fiefdom
of the mayor and his trusted associates. By this time the
mayor, if he is of at least average ability, will have a firm
political base for his next move: a seat on the provincial
council. Dealings at this level grow enormously in complexity; for provincial elections a mayor will need not only the
votes from his own *comune*, but also votes from many other
*comuni* where he may not be known. The only way to
achieve this is through the party machinery. In neighbouring
towns the local party will give instructions to its troops as to

who should get their second-preference votes. As elections to the provincial council are also based on proportional representation, the transfer of second-preference votes is crucial. An ambitious man can work his way from provincial, to regional, to national government. Each step needs carefully constructed alliances, an astute estimation of who is important and therefore to be cultivated, and an ability to feel no remorse for those who can no longer be of help. By this means Italy fills its upper houses of the legislature with the quality of people it deserves.

And what of the honest man? As a political species he is endangered but not quite extinct. The problem facing him is that the political arena is an inhospitable habitat. If an honest man accepts no bribes, how can he hope to influence those who do? Where will he get the money? Certainly at local level, where the relationship between the voters and the elected is incestuously close, his problems are huge. Suppose this honest councillor objects at a council meeting to a planning proposal that he feels is wrong; the proposal will be blocked. After the meeting the mayor will be asked by the applicant what transpired. 'It would have been passed,' says the mayor, 'but Tizio blocked the proposal.' So Tizio loses votes at the next election. If he blocks any more proposals, he will lose still more votes. If he never gets elected again, none of his ideals or his honest approach will influence council meetings. The strategy of an honest man must be of infinite subtlety if he is ever to have an effect on Italian political life.

That such men undoubtedly exist despite the system is a testament to man's indomitable hope. The brave men who knowingly risk their lives by becoming judges or prosecutors in Sicily's anti-Mafia campaign may be few in number, but at least they prove that the whole of the body politic is not yet infected. It is possible that Giuseppe Falcone's murder by the Mafia might ignite in the Italian people an urge to reform the system and perhaps look more closely at the kind of individuals who present themselves for election.

# 9

## *Clean Hands*

It's not often that momentous changes can be pinned down as stemming from one specific event in history. Caesar crossing the Rubicon and the conversion of Constantine spring to mind, but little else. The breaching of the Berlin Wall has created changes throughout Europe that will continue to ripple for years. In Italy it could be said to have caused a revolution and the creation of the Second Republic.

Since the end of the Second World War the Christian Democrat Party has had an uninterrupted span of government. The reason for this is simple: the only alternative for the electorate was the Communist Party. As the largest opposition party, they were seen as a threat not only by the ruling élite, but also by the Americans. In the years immediately following the war millions of dollars were channelled into Italy overtly by way of loans and grants for rebuilding the war-damaged economy, but also covertly through the CIA, whose express aim was to keep the Communists from power. Gladio, a secret cellular network, was set up with CIA help after the war. Each cell was made up of three people – an officer and two others. No cell knew the members of any other cell; only the area commander knew the officers of the cells under his command. One of these well-armed, expressly anti-Communist cells was made up of my father, his cousin Dino and his uncle Antonio. In the event of a threatened Communist take-over, Gladio would be put into action – this despite the fact that secret societies were officially forbidden by the state.

As their name suggests, the Christian Democrats, ever since they were founded, have been closely allied to the Catholic Church. As with similar European parties, the main planks of their credo were family values and anti-Communist fervour. In this, at least, they were at one with the Church. This bipolar axis was augmented by a further accommodation with the Mafia in Sicily and the Camorra in Naples. Crudely speaking, this alliance had money to buy support through patronage, moral authority from the pulpit, and, with its links with the underworld, the means of policing its friends and enemies. Just as at local level a mayor increases his power with his length of tenure, the Christian Democrats built up an edifice that until recently seemed impregnable. Effectively Italy had a one-party state that dispensed jobs and government contracts to its friends and created difficulties and obstacles for its enemies.

Italians were well aware of the corruption in government. Everyone had been party to it to some degree or other. That their politicians were on the make was a self-evident truth; no one doubted it. It was reluctantly accepted by many as the price to be paid to keep the system functioning and the Communists out of power. The fact is that for perhaps the majority of Italians this Augean stable of corruption was not just the best of a bad lot, it was a system that brought prosperity. By 1989 Italy could rank itself fourth in the world's developed economies as measured by gross domestic product. All over the country evidence of this prosperity was there to see. Not only were large civic projects started and sometimes even finished, but the staggering waste of money in almost all ventures was seen in itself as evidence of the vast wealth of the state. Most middle-class Italians had two or three houses, at least two cars, their children had motor bikes, their houses were filled with all the latest high technology.

The boom was explosive. Families who had been chronically poor for generations had money to spend. They took foreign holidays, they bought luxury goods, they took up hobbies and sports. For all the known defects of the system, it none the less provided work and prosperity.

With the fall of the Berlin Wall, the Christian Democrats lost their main justification for being in power, other than their own self-interest. Meanwhile the Communists were suffering the same swing against them as was taking place elsewhere in Europe. In a matter of months they were no longer a credible alternative government. In response they changed their name to the Democratic Left, and most of their policies as well.

In April 1992 the first cracks began to appear in the government edifice with the exit of Bettino Craxi, the Socialist prime minister. By the start of 1993 the entire superstructure had begun to collapse like a punctured tyre. What had looked so solid, so immutable, so permanent, had begun to fall apart with a rapidity that was alarming. In Sora, for decades a stronghold of the Christian Democrats, the party polled less than 1,000 votes out of 22,000 in the spring elections of 1993 and, all over Italy, support again collapsed in the autumn local elections. The four government parties together polled only 14 per cent of the vote. If it were not for the system of staggered elections in Italy, whereby only a portion of the delegates are elected at a time, it is clear that the Christian Democrats and the Socialists would be left with barely a deputy to their name after the general election of 1994 if voting patterns continued. Their rout has been virtually total; so much so that in many electoral areas anyone standing against them was almost assured of success no matter what their policies. In a still evolving revolution it is far from clear what the currents and the driving forces are. It is true, however, that the first broadsides were fired on the *ancien régime* by the judiciary.

What gave the honest man a chance to change the political morass was a dispersed but gradually growing awareness that the tide of history was on the turn. The newspaper *La Republica* was more fearless than others in continuing to report corruption and abuses of power. La Rete, a newly formed political party in Sicily that was overtly anti-Mafia, brought a new awareness to the mainland of the links between the Mafia and the establishment. Young investigative magistrates champed at the bit and did not always find as their politically appointed superiors directed. The Lombard League, the fastest growing political force, weighed in behind the investigations into corruption. The news programme on the third state television channel, TG3, was in the vanguard of bringing alternative voices and opinions into the public forum. These disparate movements were the tinder for the revolutionary fire.

Even within the establishment there was discontent on the back-benches. Deputies were increasingly aware that they were no more than a rubber-stamp legislature, that the real power was in the hands of a small coterie christened CAF by the press – Craxi, Andreotti and Forlani. The prospects of political advancement for these back-benchers were non-existent and the political wind was turning. The smart move was to be on the side of change. Mario Segni was the first Christian Democrat to jump ship with a group of followers and set himself firmly outside the existing power bloc, thus probably ensuring his political survival.

In Sicily the balance of power had shifted. Huge profits from the heroin trade had swelled the coffers of the Mafia to the point that they now had more money and more guns at their command than the politicians. This was demonstrated to the government and the public by the murders in Sicily of anti-Mafia judges Falcone and Borsellino. For once everyone was agreed – something had to be done.

The Church's authority and its respect from the faithful

was also haemorrhaging: no longer could the Christian Democrats assume that support from the pulpit would translate into
votes. The alliance that had served so well for so long was
unravelling. The scene was set for the revolution.

Antonio di Pietro headed the investigation into corruption
in Milan. One of his first acts was to issue all the members of
his team with portable computers. All their files were kept on
disk and always on their persons. Theft of documentation, a
constant problem during previous investigations, was avoided.
His investigations have crept relentlessly and fearlessly up the
political ladder. Currently he is snapping at the heels of
Craxi. Since his investigations began, di Pietro has been
lionized by the press; his name is spoken with respect in every
bar. He is honest, and is being cast in the role of saviour of
the people.

The effect of these investigations has been to reinvigorate
the judiciary. Once the docile lap-dogs of the politicians, they
are rediscovering their power and their purpose. All over
Italy the prefectures are doing what was once inconceivable –
they are investigating all levels of government, thoroughly
and decisively. Suddenly politicians from local to national
government are being handcuffed and locked up pending
their hearings. Italy's none-too-salubrious gaols are now holding men in Armani suits and Gucci shoes. Many of them find
their new position so intolerable that after a few hours they
beg to make a voluntary statement to the magistrates incrimi-
nating everyone they know. Many have simply committed
suicide rather than go through the due process. Like the witch
trials of the sixteenth century, each confession brings new
investigations. The judges' campaign has been christened *mani
pulite* – clean hands.

As usual in Italy, nothing is entirely clear. The state appara-
tus is not sitting idly by while its world collapses around it.
By late 1993, more than a year after the main thrust of the
investigations had begun, stories have emerged of judges who

have taken bribes. This is clearly intended by the establishment to dull the edge of the *mani pulite* campaign by implying that the investigative magistrates are as corrupt as those they are investigating. It is commonly accepted in local bars that the strange spate of terrorist bombings in the summer of 1993 were state-inspired, their purpose being to shift media attention from the corruption investigations. So far these manoeuvres have not stopped the relentless probing.

The problem that will have to be addressed is that no one has spotlessly clean hands. It was impossible to live in Italy and not be tainted in some way by the pandemic corruption that has existed for the last half century. Most people who have a job today owe it to some kind of *raccomandazione*, a recommendation accompanied by implicit or explicit emoluments. That was the way it worked. Whether it was to your liking or not, to survive you had to play by the rules. Ultimately recriminations will have to be based not simply on infractions of the letter of the law but rather on the degree of abuse. Clearly there are those who have worked the system not solely because it was there, but with self-interest as their sole motivation. By late 1993 Carlo de Benedetti, the head of Olivetti, was arrested and subsequently released. He is a good example of where and how investigations should proceed, since he has been in the forefront of the calls for change. He was arrested, albeit briefly, on charges of paying money illegally to political parties, something he readily admitted to, since it was impossible to keep Olivetti trading without doing so. It is clear that those who worked within the corrupt system to survive cannot be bundled into the same category as those who created and ran the corruption.

Italians are sanguine about this. They say that a man who collects honey will lick his fingers. In their hearts they know that they would behave no differently. What irks, now that the carcass of the First Republic is exposed to scrutiny, is the certain knowledge that the huge state deficit that has been created can only be paid for by the average citizen. Those who have defrauded the state of millions of pounds will almost certainly be left to enjoy their spoils. The Italian parliament has even debated a proposition that would give an amnesty to any malfeasance perpetrated before 1989 – a simple expedient that would allow the legislature to legalize their many and compound crimes.

How the deficit has been created is remarkably simple. It appears that for practically every government contract the deal went like this. A new bridge is needed; the government, in the shape of the man who will sign the contract, approaches a builder. It will cost £10 million. The contract is then agreed for a greater sum, and the builder makes a large donation to the coffers of the party. Easy. As long as the money circulated within the Italian economy it appeared to work. When it started finding its way abroad in increasingly large amounts the fissures became apparent and the system teetered towards collapse. The amount of money that flowed into party coffers by this means in the good years is awe-inspiring. Unfortunately for all the major parties, by 1993 donations elicited by the old means had dried up and they found themselves virtually bankrupt, to the delight of many embittered taxpayers.

Political debate currently centres on the mechanics of the new republic. Complicated formulas involving proportional representation and first–past–the–post elections are under discussion. As with the German model, parties that poll less than 5 per cent nationally will now have no deputies in parliament, eliminating a lot of the tiny splinter groups. These proposed changes will affect all four tiers of government, and most of the changes can only be for the better.

The general revulsion Italians feel now that so many scandals have been exposed extends to Sicily and its attitude to the Mafia. The autumn elections of 1993 put Leoluca Orlando, founder of the anti-Mafia party La Rete, into power in

Palermo. All over Sicily his party has swept into town halls, changing for ever a fifty-year status quo.

All over Italy the structure of the new Second Republic will bring considerable changes at local level. Most importantly, a mayor can have only two terms of office – an eight-year reign. This one change will do more to stem the creation of feudal baronies in the *comuni* than anything else. In the first term of office a new mayor will have all the enthusiasm and purpose of a neophyte. In the second term he will not be dependent on doing favours to get votes, since he will not be able to re-present himself. This alone will clean up local politics and will certainly have a grass-roots effect on the upper levels of government. The only quibble I have with this is that it is not retrospective. So a mayor who has already been in power for twenty years or more can have another eight from the next election.

In Gallinaro *mani pulite* has brought changes. In 1993 the mayor of twenty-two years, Alberto Cassale, was removed from his post as mayor and as a provincial councillor by the prefecture in Frosinone. The reason for this was almost a trifle – the granting of planning permission for a new chemist shop on the *superstrada* that passes through the *comune* of Gallinaro, owned by my cousin Cesidio. Athough in itself a very minor infraction of the law, since the shop should have been in the town centre, it was sufficient to cause his removal from office. My first cousin, Luigi Tullio, has replaced him.

Other investigations into Gallinaro's administration are still pending, mostly relating to the disbursal of the earthquake rebuilding funds, which by 1993 totalled some 15 billion lire, about £7 million. These investigations were put in motion by the three opposition councillors, who made a *denuncia*, a formal complaint, to the magistrature. Where once complaints like these simply disappeared into a quagmire of paper, the new ethos of honesty and transparency in government has ensured that they are pursued and investigated. After nearly fifty years of quiescent magistrátes this has come as a shock. To discover that what has always been acceptable behaviour is actually against the law has caught many administrations on the hop. The plea that 'we've always done it like this' goes unheeded.

The new openness has made its first few tentative steps in Gallinaro. Under my cousin's aegis the town hall now places a copy of its agenda for council meetings on public display. All are welcome to attend. Even the opposition councillors, who include my old friends Silvano Tanzilli and Antonio Appruzzese, feel that a new era is dawning. They are given access to information that was once kept from them. The word in vogue is *trasparenza*. The divisions that had so bitterly split the town are healing beneath the genuinely kind smile of my cousin. Where discord was the rule, a new sense of common purpose seems to be evolving. The opposition councillors are even prepared to give my cousin a honeymoon period of some six months to see if he is a creature of a different colour from his predecessor.

The previous mayor, Alberto, has left a legacy of distrust and enmity which Gigino, as Luigi is known, will have to redress. The main division is between the town itself, the *centro storico*, and the rest of the *comune* where Alberto's main support came from. Almost wilfully, Alberto allowed the old town centre to decline. No attempt was made to keep traders from leaving for the greener pastures of the *superstrada*. Clementina's butcher's shop is about to close, so is Ida's hardware shop, and Sinella is even talking of closing the bar. This last would be catastrophic for the town centre. With no focus for social interaction, the town will simply become a dormitory for those who work and play elsewhere. The declining numbers who return in the summer will have nowhere to meet. These trends are not irreversible. With a little good will and vision, the town hall could do a lot to revive the town centre. What is needed is the will to do so.

The change in the government's finances will have a big impact on the *comuni* of Italy in the next few years. The big problem facing the *comuni* is *fuori bilancia* expenditure – sums not accounted for within the normal budget since it was always supposed that they would be paid for by central government. It is increasingly unlikely that this will be the case, so the citizens of each *comune* will have to pay through increases in the house taxes (there are three). Of all the prospects on the horizon, this is probably the most frightening for taxpayers. Only now are they discovering that grandiose projects such as large floodlit football pitches in mountain villages have not actually been paid for. Lavish sports facilities that are barely used will now be billed to the town's citizens. The realization that higher taxes will have to be paid to put the balance sheet right is a source of horror for most Italians.

It is this that has caused the Italians' pervasive rage in 1993. The slow understanding that they have all been ripped-off by their politicians is causing profound resentment. Politicians have been hounded and stoned in the streets by their angry constituents, they have been forced to leave restaurants, they are heckled and insulted wherever they go. Unfortunately, as yet, there is no mechanism in Italian law whereby the stolen money can be recovered. What rankles is that the very architects of the economic chaos will be able to live happily on their ill-gotten piles of loot, at worst in the exile of an off-shore tax haven.

The shortage of cash is already being felt in Gallinaro. The August *festa* of San Gerardo was a far more subdued affair in 1993 than it has been in the past. The main contributors – the emigrants in Belgium, the local businesses and inhabitants, and the regional funds – are all under financial strain. Despite the lack of funding, once again Gallinaro and San Donato hosted a conference on emigration for nearly 600 people, all of whom were fed a six-course meal in the local hotel; £9,000 was spent on this. For the first time in the three years this conference has been held questions were asked – and not just by me – as to whether in the current economic circumstances simply eating what money is left makes any sense.

A new sense of realism is emerging, a gradual realization that money spent by the state and its agents is money raised by taxation. Italians are coming to understand that the more the state spends, the more taxes you pay. When *comuni* like Gallinaro start to try to find ways of reducing their electricity bill, it is clear that a new ethos of stricter housekeeping has arrived. The days of cathedrals in the desert are at an end.

Hand in hand with better accounting is the new tax regime. For years Italians have been taxed indirectly. Now tax on income that actually bites is an ever nearer reality. The ubiquitous receipts that are foisted upon you for every purchase in a shop have become obligatory for professionals. Doctors and dentists are obliged to give them; theoretically they will have to pay tax on receipted income. Unfortunately in practice it is not working out like that. Professionals very rarely offer a receipt and asking for one has its drawbacks. If you force the issue, you are likely to find it difficult next time you need an appointment. Rather than run this very real risk, most people accept no receipt, or will settle for one that details at most a quarter of the sum actually spent.

To overcome problems such as these, now that the state has assessed the floor area of every house in Italy for the house tax, the tax collectors are applying similar formulas. If you own a house of a particular floor area, it is assumed your income cannot be less than a particular amount. Similarly, if your office is of a certain size, then your turnover is assumed to be in direct proportion. These are crude instruments and often unfair, but they will go some way towards evening the tax burden.

The problem with restructuring the tax laws is speed. All this has happened with alarming haste. In August 1993, Italy had 192 separate taxes and duties, each with its own paperwork and each adopting a different method of payment. No tax in Italy can be paid by a cheque in the post. They are payable only in cash, some at the post office, some at a bank, and some at a government bureau. To pay VAT a trader, or someone on his behalf, must spend a day queueing in the bank to hand over cash. Since the majority of traders are attempting to pay on the same day the chaos is predictable. The annual tax return document of 1993 ran to forty-eight pages and was incomprehensible to virtually everyone. Even the president declared it to have been designed by a sadistic maniac and promised that next year's will be simpler. As with most laws in Italy, the tax laws are far from clear. No one is completely certain that they have paid the required amount – there is a lingering uncertainty that some day the amounts will be re-assessed and large fines will be levied.

The shock to the system is considerable. Up to now taxes have been moderate and often collected haphazardly. Many professionals and traders have paid little if anything, and are unused to the idea of taxation. Suddenly, within the span of a year, their world has been turned on its head. Not only are taxes being demanded, they are being collected with a vigour as never before. The taxes on houses will certainly rise in the next few years. People who have several houses, and they are many, will find that the expense will outweigh the benefits of keeping more than one house. As more people try to sell them, the property market will suffer as well. All over Italy workers returning from the summer break have found the factory gates closed. As unemployment begins to rocket, Black Autumn is living up to its name. The immediate future is far from rosy.

One spin-off from the house taxes should be a decrease in, or possibly the end of, speculative building. Up to now building a house was a sound investment. The proof is the sheer quantity of them in various stages of construction around the place. I was given figures from a housing census which show that there is housing for 80,000 in the Comino Valley, whose actual population is around 19,000. The difference cannot be explained by people like me, who do not live permanently in their houses, since any householder is counted on the electoral register. There are simply many more houses than there are people to occupy them. The building continues, but it would be my bet that when market forces begin to be felt, the concreting of the valley will eventually end.

It is hard not to be optimistic about the current turmoil. Whether it all works out as planned or not, it will still be preferable to what went before. Changes to the system appear to be radical, and should have far-reaching effects. It should, however, be borne in mind that the people discussing the changes, the legislators, are those who have most benefited from the previous arrangements. It is difficult to imagine greedy and venal people voting short rations for themselves. Most likely the changes will be made when a new political force with new members, such as the Lombard League, comes to power. If the collapse of the Christian Democrat party continues, the next elections will certainly see them out of office, and possibly reduced to a rump of members.

These are turbulent times in Italy and only the brave venture prophecies, but it seems clear that the Second Republic will start life with new political alliances and a new set of deputies who will at least profess to have *mani pulite*. Whether whoever governs Italy in the next five years can keep the economy on an even keel and avert a tax-payers' revolution is anyone's guess. Current trends point to violent revolution – but then in Italy they always have.

# 10

# *Walking to Sinella's*

Gallinaro is not beautiful. Centuries of poverty, *miseria*, have left the old town centre dilapidated and to some degree devoid of permanent inhabitants. The newly built part of the town is essentially graceless, even though large amounts of foreign-earned capital have been lavished upon it. The prosperity of recent years has not passed Gallinaro by, but the Italian urge for the new has left it possibly more impoverished. What was typical of traditional stonework, or of historic or local interest, has mostly been removed, broken or covered in concrete. This disregard for the old is not peculiar to Gallinaro, but is endemic in the south of Italy. What to a tourist is a fascinating relic of the sixteenth century is to the inhabitants a reminder of hardship, grinding poverty and a life of discomfort and hard work. A brand new house of poured concrete is perceived as infinitely superior to a restored ruin, a roof of new tiles is preferable to leaking roman *canali*. And yet, despite all the unsympathetic alterations and reconstructions, the village still retains the quintessential qualities of an Italian hill-town: it is picturesque, and to me it's home.

A walk from the Atina side of Gallinaro to the other takes about fifteen minutes at a dawdle. The road follows the crest of the hill on which the town is built. At the road sign welcoming you to Gallinaro, which also informs you that you are some 600 metres above sea-level, a chain-link fence lines the road on the right. Behind this six-foot fence zebras and ostriches frequently browse. This is the upper boundary of Don Armando Mancini's estate. Enormous by Italian standards, it runs from the eastern valley floor all the way up to Gallinaro town, taking in several small valleys and forests. It is surrounded by high fences and is strictly out of bounds to all. Don Armando is indisputably the valley's Mr Big. He dominates the building trade in the valley and to a large extent the province too. His influence is keenly felt in the administrations of nearly all the valley towns, the province, and some would maintain Rome as well. He is a man to respect.

Following the road brings you to the beginning of Gallinaro new-town. In June and July this stretch of road is alive at night with fireflies that flit and bustle in their mating-dance. On both sides of the road there are large villas, shuttered for eleven months of the year, their owners in France or Belgium. Taking up the ground floor and garden of one of these villas is Maurizio's *pizzeria*, which serves possibly the finest pizzas available for 30 kilometres in any direction. Maurizio and his Canadian wife Maria make the real thing, in a brick, domed oven fired by beech and oak. This is probably the only place in Gallinaro where you can see people from other towns, the closest thing we have to tourism. Even in the winter, when all life appears to be hibernating, people find their way here. Like most Gallinarese, Maurizio's family make good cabernet-based wine, and he is not shy in suggesting it as an accompaniment to his pizzas.

A little further along, on the left is the town hall, the *comune*. It is housed in the old school building while the new *comune* is being built, of which more anon. Opposite the town hall, in a place that appears curiously inappropriate, is a new bar. Not surprisingly, it is frequented by the denizens of the town hall, and, less surprising still, has begun to be the preferred choice of the administration. This has had a polarizing effect on the town. Until recently Sinella's was the only bar, apart from a couple of dingy shebeens. Regardless of politics, this was where the village met for coffee, for recreation. Now the choice of bar is almost a political statement. The mayor lives near the town hall, he and his associates meet in the bar there, and the bulk of his sustaining votes come from here. The citizens of the old town feel abandoned and ignored, further increasing their likelihood of voting against the administration, and consequently ensuring that their needs and wants are barely addressed.

Last summer I found myself doubting this analysis. All through August the mayor and many of his councillors were to be seen in Bar Sinella, in the heart of the old town. Had a truce been agreed? It turned out there was a simpler explanation. A new law was proposed last year granting voting rights to Italians living outside Italy. For the last couple of years I have received from the *comune* of Gallinaro a voting slip for each election – provincial, regional and national – sent to me in Ireland. The Italian state will pay for my travel to Italy, as long as it is by train, to enable me to vote. It doesn't take much calculation to see that this could become very expensive. The new law allows voting in the country of domicile, even for local elections. Gallinaro's emigrants, far more numerous than its inhabitants, are now voters, which explains the courtship of the emigrants by the current administration.

Far-sighted local administrators are assiduously cultivating the enormous block of new voters. The next local elections in Gallinaro are not until 1995, but preparations are being made now. As well as three lavish conferences to discuss the needs of the emigrant community, Italians who choose to return to Italy will have their moving expenses largely paid for; there are schools specifically for the children of emigrants where the emphasis is on learning Italian before the children transfer to a normal school; housing is available for those who cannot afford to buy – in short, a whole panoply of support.

Whether or not all this can be maintained in the current climate of severe austerity remains to be seen.

Beyond the town hall is the Sanctuary of San Gerardo. The church dates from the twelfth century, although the bulk of the structure is more recent.

Opposite the Sanctuary the road is flanked by a low wall, where the whole western half of the valley is on view. Below this point is the little Chapel of the Baby Jesus. In front of the Sanctuary is the largest open space in the town. It is not a piazza, but a place where the buses bringing pilgrims park. Nestling between two large rubbish bins and a specialized bin for medicines and batteries is one of the few remaining public fountains in the town. Most of the time the area surrounding the fountain and the bins has more litter than the bins hold.

This open space is one of the few spots in the village with a view of both halves of the valley. Settefrati, the highest of the towns, clings to the valley sides, further east is Picinisco, described by D. H. Lawrence in *The Lost Girl*; at the far end is San Biagio, and below it and nearer is Villa Latina. From here you can also see Gallinaro's oldest established night-club, Smeralda's. What little crime there is in the village is allegedly caused by some of the less desirable elements who come from Cassino and Sora to patronize the night-club. Along the bottom of the hill running north to south is the *superstrada*, a wide road connecting Atina to San Donato.

All over Italy hill-towns are suffering the same fate. The reason for their positioning – security from marauding bandits – has long gone. Their inconvenience, however, remains. Atina is a long way towards moving from the hill-top to the plain below. Frosinone town has long since completed the transposition, Gallinaro is beginning it. Most of the town's main retail outlets – the supermarket, the chemist, the builders' suppliers – have all moved to the valley, flanking the road. The hotel is here, as are another two night-clubs, furniture shops, cafés and restaurants. It is easy to imagine a time not long from now when the hill-top will be a dormitory, and commercial and social life will be down in the valley.

Dominating the open space in front of the Sanctuary of San Gerardo is one of the town's hillocks. The old road skirts it to the east, and a new one circles it to the west, joining the old road some 200 metres further on. Two buildings top this rise, one the school, and the other the fine house of the ex-schoolmaster, Crescenzo Tanzilli. What purpose the new road? At the back of this crest the skeleton of the new town hall moulders. Like most new buildings in this seismic area, it is built of poured concrete. Like some child's building toy, the uprights and cross-pieces are shuttered and poured, until a skeleton building is made. At this point the sides are filled in, windows and doors placed, and the roof tiled. The new town hall, however, will certainly remain in the skeletal stage for the foreseeable future. The funds from central coffers arrived for building both the access road and the town hall, but somehow the money just wasn't enough and no more is forthcoming. Where the money went can only be surmised, but what was a lovely hillock is now despoiled.

Where this pointless new road rejoins the old is the beginning of the climb to the old centre. Probably the only monument to Fascist endeavour still extant in Gallinaro is the viaduct which carries the road at an even incline over what was a steep gully impenetrable to motor traffic; before its construction the village had effectively only one access road – the one from the other end. Apart from making the expansion of the town in this direction possible, the viaduct had an extraordinary effect on the houses on either side. Their front doors used to give on to the old track in the gully, but when the viaduct was built what were once bedrooms became the main entrance, accessed by tiny bridges from the sides of the viaduct. I've never been inside any of these houses, but internally they must be upside-down by any standards.

The top of the viaduct brings the road alongside the main

square, Piazza Santa Maria. Even for the Comino Valley this is a sorry sight. A previous administration created it by the simple expedient of allowing three garages to be built into the hillside, with the stipulation that their roofs would become part of an enlarged and levelled piazza. Two sides of the piazza are bounded by once-proud *palazzi*, one of which seems about to collapse at any moment. Until recently, it was the town hall. The south side is a monument to the newly arrived concept of conservation. The Church of Santa Maria, unquestionably the least architecturally interesting of the town's churches, is now a preserved ruin. Alongside it is the poured concrete monstrosity of the recently erected war memorial. Thankfully, none of this can be seen from the road, so the assault on the eye and sensibilities can be avoided.

The road climbs more gently at this point, passing on the right two of the few shops that have not defected to the valley, and on the left a low wall allowing an unhindered view to the west. Look over the wall and a large expanse of concrete presents itself. This is in fact the second story of the projected new piazza. Because Gallinaro is built along the crest of a hill, there is almost no level ground, so it must be created. Built into the steep slope, another concrete skeleton supports this area of about 30 by 20 metres. This, too, will never be finished. The allocated funds arrived and somehow just weren't enough to finish the job. The cost of this concrete skeleton so far? £250,000.

Some 50 metres further on, evidence of the 1984 earthquake comes into view – not the destruction it caused, but the ghastly effects of letting Italians loose to rebuild. The vast expanse of plain concrete retaining-wall may well serve a purpose other than a rubbish tip and occasional park- ing place, but this is functionalism devoid of any aesthetic merit. A few more paces brings you past a couple more houses to the public garden, which adjoins my house. It has recently been bought by the *comune* for use as a playground,

although swings, roundabouts and slides have never materialized. It is home, however, to rubbish bins, and is now the
focus of a campaign to make the administration figuratively
and literally clean up its act.

From this point the road begins its descent, passing my
house on the left, and the backs of some old houses on the
right. They were part of the old walled town, the backs of
the houses forming the medieval walls. Just below these
houses is the old-town piazza. It is tiny, and marks what was
once a gate into the medieval town. Until 1945 it was
considerably larger, but in the chaos immediately after the
war planning permission was granted for a house right in the
middle of the piazza.

This is where I would want to bring any visitor to see
Gallinaro as it should be. All the old houses have been painted
in pastel shades, the restoration work done with some care.
Although a purist could find cause for complaint, the houses
are pretty and the general effect is pleasing and picturesque.
Until recently there was a stone in the square, roughly cubic,
once used by debtors. To proclaim bankruptcy, the debtor
would remove his trousers and sit on the stone, the origin of a
crude dialect phrase for going bankrupt. From this tiny
square you can look up to the main church, taking in most of
the old town as well; and looking down the long, thin piazza,
which originally formed the centre of the old walled town,
you can see the men at the café tables shouting and gesticulating as they play cards. Of all the images that I hold of this
village, it is the ones from here that give me the most
pleasure.

This was the part of the town most affected by the earthquake, the houses being old and in poor condition. Consequently this is where the bulk of the rebuilding has happened.
The argument rages still about the rebuilding. Our neighbouring town, San Donato, managed to restore its old buildings
leaving the old stonework façades intact. In Gallinaro the

exteriors have had steel mesh riveted to them and have been covered in a cement render. It's effective and cheap, but some of the more beautiful old stonework is now under an inch of sand and cement.

Despite my misgivings about the effect of the rebuilding on the village as a whole, at a personal level I have been fortunate. Like most old houses in Gallinaro, mine was fitted with chains after the 1921 earthquake. A house in an earthquake opens out like an artichoke, from the top. To counteract this, the upper levels were threaded with chains which bound opposite walls to one another. Although this work stopped the house from collapsing, it was damaged extensively and was one of the first to benefit from the rebuilding. Without filling in any forms, without making applications to government offices, the local administration simply rebuilt it. The work done was extensive: a new tiled roof; a reinforced concrete cordon around the top of the walls; the interior of the upper storey lined with steel mesh and rendered; the supporting walls and arches in the *cantina* buttressed and strengthened. As it stands now, the house should withstand all but the worst geological violence.

I was frankly amazed at the extent of the work and its quality. I found Alberto, the then mayor, and thanked him.

He looked at me quizzically. 'You're serious, aren't you?'

'Of course. It's a good job.'

'Well, you're the first person in the village to have no complaints. Everyone else has been moaning about the mess the builders left.'

This was in 1987. The previous year my house in Ireland had been under a metre of water as a result of Hurricane Charlie. There was no help available from government, council or insurance. Returning to Italy to find my house restored by the administration made comparisons inevitable, and whatever mess had been left by the builders seemed a small inconvenience to me. There is a lot to be said for living in a country with a large base of taxpayers.

The area around the main church is a maze of narrow alleys. Most of the houses here date from the twelfth century. One of the peculiarities of ownership has caused immense problems for the rebuilding. Almost nowhere in Gallinaro is a house owned by one family. What the Gallinarese refer to as a *casa*, a house, in fact means a place to live. Especially in the *centro storico*, flying freehold is the norm. One apartment runs in a long strip along four houses. The apartments can be large, on several floors, but they rarely mirror the divisions in the external façade. This is the result of centuries of dividing houses between offspring, and of people's willingness to sell single rooms to abutting houses. Last year I was offered the top room of the house adjoining mine. The owners have a problem: the house has been abandoned for years, but now that it has been rebuilt by the earthquake fund, the two brothers and one sister cannot agree on how to sell it. There are four rooms, one above the other. It is clearly impossible for each of them to have a separate entrance to their respective floors, so one alternative is to sell it, room by room, to the neighbours.

Beyond the main church the road descends gently towards San Donato, a few scattered *contratti*, or hamlets, along the way. The *campo santo*, the town cemetery, is on the left. It has high walls and a large, iron double gate. Inside are my ancestors, their names and dates carefully recorded on the graves. This is where my father lies buried and where an empty space awaits me. The custom here is not to inter the dead, but to place the coffins on large shelves stacked four-high which surround the cemetery wall on the inside. Marble face-plates close in the coffin and record the name and dates of the body within. Most graves carry a photograph as well, as a memento for the living. There is a matter-of-factness about the system which reflects the closeness to the birth and death cycle that all country-dwellers have. When the next death in the family comes, the shelf that has been occupied the longest is opened; the remains are placed in an urn and the urn joins the others on the top shelf, the name being added to that face-plate while a new one marks the details of the recent arrival. With this system a family vault of five places – four stacked high and one below ground at the base – can serve for many generations whilst saving precious space. The habit of entombing above ground is a function of the difficulty of interring in rocky land. I have a vivid memory of a visit to Brancaleone in Calabria many years ago. The old town was abandoned on a hill-top while the new bustled at the sea shore. Earthquakes had shaken the graves and many of the cover plates were cracked and broken, exposing the occupants. Inside several of them were skeletons with rotting clothing, but with perfect leather boots.

The Gallinaro cemetery is disturbing for me since I once walked around it calculating the age of Tullio males: very few survived longer than sixty years. Perhaps it was no more than their tough, back-breaking life taking its toll.

The *comune* of Gallinaro extends almost the same distance from each side of the road and accounts for roughly half of the official population. The town centre, once the commercial nub and on Sundays the social nub, is going through a transformation. Today all the inhabitants have a car, they shop in the big supermarkets either on the *superstrada* or in large towns. Sunday mass is not the draw it was, and anyway the main church has been closed since the earthquake. The patterns of behaviour that created a vibrant town centre are changing. People are dispersed, they work in Sora or Cassino, they have friends in other towns, they have transport. The little villages of the Comino Valley worked when their economy was peasant. You walked in the morning to your patch of earth, worked it, and walked home at dusk. Until recently there were many who had never travelled beyond the valley. It was a self-sufficient society, almost apart from the rest of Italy. D. H. Lawrence described the valley as 'a world within a world, a valley of many hills and townlets and streams shut in beyond access'. The ancient patterns of life have been eradicated in the last forty years and with it the very reasons for the structure and shape of the villages. Already the majority of the houses in Gallinaro are empty for eleven months of the year, owned by emigrants who come in August, or by Gallinarese who work in Rome or Milan, who return to see old friends and rediscover their roots.

Quite where this trend will lead I'm not sure. Long-forgotten owners of abandoned houses which have been rebuilt from central coffers have surfaced, and many of the houses are now for sale. Who will buy them? Already we have a family of Romans who have no prior connections with the village – they came because it is beautiful, because the air is clean, and to get out of Rome in the summer. I would guess that more and more urban Italians will buy holiday homes in small villages like ours to escape their own form of rat-race and to rediscover in a small rural community some of the old pleasures and values that they have missed.

Two years ago we stopped for the night on our way to Ireland in Castle Combe, in Wiltshire. This village is absurdly pretty, and looks in danger to me of becoming a theme park. Everyone we met seemed to have moved from London. The pubs and the Castle itself are owned by anonymous and amorphous conglomerates. It seems to be a rural backdrop, a theatrical set against which temporary visitors strut and fret their hour and then are seen no more. Gallinaro may be a long way from this, but the thought remains. One of the main topics of conversation amongst the emigrants is the relationship that their children have with the town. Many of these emigrants have elderly relatives still living in the village, so it is partly to visit them that they return. Their children, especially the teenagers, would for the most part much prefer to be in Torremolinos, or anywhere rather than rural Italy. For the bucolic there is much on offer, but Euro-teenagers want more than this village can provide.

For the moment the glue that holds the centre together is provided by Sinella. Cesidio Franciosa, known universally as Sinella, owns the bar of the same name. It is home to the disgruntled voters of the old town, the opposition parties, and all the holiday-makers who know nothing of the political undercurrents.

I have never seen Sinella with anything other than a cheery smile. During the summer he works insanely long hours, serving until two or three in the morning, and re-opening at seven in the morning. In the winter he keeps it open and warm all day long while the old men sit, smoke and play cards, ordering a coffee every five hours or so. There is a definite touch of the classical in the names of the regulars: Othello, Pompey, Attila, Dionysius, Augustus, Maximus, Achilles, Horace and Hercules all play cards here.

It's hard to believe how cold it gets in January and February, especially if your memories are only of summer. For eight consecutive years we spent the winter in Gallinaro. Had we been tied to the village with no transport, there would have been literally nothing to do to while away the hours outside our house other than sit in Sinella's. As it was, we took to skiing, against the advice of everyone over fifty, who explained that the mountain air made you sick. Anyone under fifty thought that we were eccentric, so our activities were largely ignored. Still, it eventually caught on and the village now has a thriving ski club.

During the summer Sinella comes into his own. He is one of those people whose enthusiasm for life is infectious. He organizes music and dancing in the little piazza outside his bar, despite the obstacles that the administration put in his way. I honestly believe he should be rewarded for performing a public service.

At one end of the piazza, just outside the bar, are a flight of steps made of local marble which lead up towards the church. These steps serve as a dais for the musicians when

Sinella organizes an evening's entertainment. Like most Italians south of Rome he loves Neapolitan songs and music, so that is what we tend to get. One of the regulars in the bar is Franco la Sip. Because he used to work for the phone company, SIP, that has become his name. He is a Neapolitan who has now settled in Gallinaro the better to play cards, and, because of his connections, he finds us good Neapolitan musicians to play. Both Franco and Sinella have fine tenor voices and both of them sing when there is a PA system available.

The little piazza is like an outdoor salon in the summer; it is sheltered from the wind and the full sun, and there are benches under the oleanders that line its sides. When the construction companies that did the rebuilding finished in this section, as a gift to the village they re-paved the piazza in a sort of red, patterned cobble. This, combined with fact that here is one of the few places in the village where nothing offends the eye, makes outside Sinella's a good place to sit.

On 12 August 1991 Sinella and Franco between them organized supper for the whole village. Trestle tables ran the length of the piazza, ready to accommodate 200 diners. Opposite the bar Franco had set up his outdoor kitchen, where he cooked the pasta and meat. We were all to arrive at eight with our own crockery, cutlery and wine; the food was Franco's job.

One of the joys of living in Italy is the fact that it is possible to organize an outdoor event in advance and know that rain will not stop play. We walked across the road from our house to the little piazza clutching one bottle of Nicola's rosé and one of Gerardo's white. A gibbous moon hung high overhead and a warm breeze rustled the oleanders. A group of friends had laid siege to a centre table and had kept us a place. As we tasted each other's wine we waited to see what was in store. I found the whole idea of a meal for a village just wonderful and tried to photograph it. Unfortunately the shutter jammed, so I have no photographs of that night.

Franco came by, shouting, barracking, fencing with heck-lers. Before each of us he dropped a plastic plate with home-made bread and *prosciutto*. 'Nine courses to come!' he yelled over his shoulder.

We had paid 10,000 lire each for this, about £5. Even assuming this to be a non-profit-making venture, already no easy assumption where Franco is involved, it seemed absurdly cheap for ten courses. OK, in the end the courses were not huge, and coffee counted as one too, but it was one of the most memorable nights that I have spent in the piazza.

After the coffee the band began to set up and a space was cleared for dancing. For me it was not the first time and hopefully it will not be the last, but there is something magical about balmy evenings, sitting outside and listening to the saccharine schmaltz of Neapolitan love songs. I love it un-ashamedly. Sinella started the dancing, a *lambada* I think, with an attractive lady from Rome. His movements fascinated me, the kind of sinuous twisting that an overdose of Dopamine produces, all curvy limbs but somehow taut. I was mesmer-ized, never having seen the like, but my wife found it a little unattractive. Anyway, it had the desired effect, for soon we were all dancing.

Once Sinella had sung *O sole mio*, the microphone became fair game for anyone who could get hold of it. The man on keyboards began to assume the haunted look of a musician who, try as he might, is unable to find the key in which to accompany the singer. By two o'clock, having tried all the keys they knew, the musicians went back to Naples. In what I thought was a miracle of organizing a crowd of happy Italians, Sinella got the piazza cleared, the trestles put away, the rubbish in sacks and the whole place back in order in less than ten minutes. Franco says he'll do it again but next time he's going to charge properly, whatever that might mean.

That Sinella is still running his bar is thanks to the Baby Jesus. As the Chapel of the Baby Jesus began to attract increasing numbers of pilgrims, Sinella opened a small shack from which he sold coffee and beer. Now it has grown hugely, one of several watering-holes provided by the village to extract cash from pilgrims. It is undoubtedly his main source of revenue and it has allowed him to keep the bar in the village going, giving us a focal point. For the sake of the village I hope he prospers.

# II

# *Sex and Fashion*

Italians enjoy public life. They are at their happiest in the centre of the crowd. This simple truth explains much of the shape of daily life. Architecturally, it ensures that all towns and villages have a piazza where their inhabitants can meet and chat. It explains why Italian houses have balconies that look out on to the road, why cafés have tables on the pavement and why Italians are content in high-density housing. It explains why Italians take so much care over their appearance, why style and fashion are so important, why fine art is so much a part of urban heritage.

At an individual level Italians define themselves in terms of their public persona; it is very much a case of 'what you see is what you get'. With strangers they are at ease, comfortable and confident. Tortured angst and self-doubt, although not unknown, are not easily discerned in the daily mêlée of Italian life. Anguished soul-searching appears to be a condition better suited to the longer, cooler winters of the North.

The ancient Romans, whose influence still pervades modern Italian life, had a name for their republic: the *res publica*, the public thing. It was not individual rights that were enshrined in early Roman law, but rather a codification of proper public behaviour. The emphasis was on social interaction rather than personal ethics and morality. Despite the appearance of chaos and disorder, the *res publica* has its own rigid codes of behaviour which are observed for the most part willingly by Italians. People who know Rome, Milan or any large Italian city will no doubt disagree with this, but this code of behaviour still applies in the provinces, and it does exist, although somewhat less apparently, in the big cities. Making sense of the seeming anarchy of daily life depends on understanding the systems that underpin the interactions.

Appearances are paramount. Even the most casual observer will notice that cars are almost always clean, shiny and unmarked. A battered and tatty jalopy will draw attention to itself, not just from onlookers but also from the police. No matter how mechanically sound it may be, it will be perceived as unroadworthy. This attitude to outward appearance applies equally to people. Until very recently there was a widespread perception that people with long hair or beards were somehow suspect, anarchic or at odds with society. In effect it became a self-fulfilling prophecy, since only those individuals who wanted to make a public statement about their political or social views grew a beard or long hair.

What this points to is that public appearance is inextricably linked in the Italian mind with the content or the form; books are judged by their covers. Mussolini understood this, and ensured that all public building under his regime was classical, noble, monumental, with an immediate impression of eternal solidity. In the minds of rural Italians the architecture of the Fascist town hall or public convenience was an outward manifestation of those same qualities possessed by their government.

Apart from making trains run on time, for which Mussolini is endlessly credited, he is famed in Italy for draining the Pontine marshes. They lay to the south of Rome, running along the coast as far south as the promontory of Circeo, the fabled home of Circe, who bewitched Odysseus. It was a wide stretch of coastal plain which represented to land-hungry Italians an opportunity for new land to cultivate. Since Roman times attempts to drain the marshes had failed, work-

ers falling prey to the endemic malaria that was carried by the large and predatory mosquitoes. In the twentieth century DDT killed the mosquitoes and the marshes were drained with mechanical diggers. When the land was sufficiently firm for building, Sabaudia, a large town, was built in less than a year as a monument to Fascist endeavour. The whole area became part of the new province of Latina.

No one these days would be so naïve as to equate architecture with propriety in government, but the tendency to equate appearance and content is strong. This is what makes Italians so fashion-conscious.

Take Italian bathrooms. Filled with the most technologically advanced taps and fittings, they leave the visitor with an impression of twentieth-century wizardry. The fact that all these gleaming designer taps are connected to fifteenth-century underground piping is concealed. Only the owner knows how often his loo backs up and overflows on to the pretty ceramic tiles. As ever, what matters is not the efficient functioning of boring old unseen plumbing, it is the visual display of thoroughly modern convenience. Apart from their extraordinary variety of taps and fittings – you need about five minutes of familiarization to find out how everything works – Italian bathrooms are an electrician's nightmare. I have seen power points placed underneath shower roses and wiring earthed to pipes – if the system is earthed at all. Once again, the latest in fashion for electrical accessories is on display, all connected to a potentially lethal electricity supply. If Italians have money to spend, it's more likely to be spent on a new car parked conspicuously in front of the house rather than on rewiring the house.

That clothes maketh the man is not an old adage in Italy, it's a way of life. As far as I know, Italians spend more per capita than anyone else on clothes. Fashion is a tyrant in Italy. If you should take it into your head to buy a blue pullover, you'd better hope that blue is one of this year's colours; if it isn't you won't find a blue pullover anywhere.

The tyranny of fashion has many guises. In clothes it is obvious and immediate: no one can afford to be seen in last year's ski wear, or in a cut that is no longer *di moda*. Italian designers have in recent years underscored this anxiety among their buyers by putting the year of manufacture prominently on the garment. Either you unpick this, leaving an ugly mark, or you buy a new one next year.

The obverse of this love of beauty is a dislike of ugliness. *Non è bello* has a definitive ring as a put down. Paradoxically, the copious hideous buildings and odorous heaps of rubbish don't seem to qualify as ugliness. The dislike of ugliness takes many forms; its most obvious is the need for even the most functional object to be designed. It is not sufficient that a can opener works well, it must do so beautifully. Until the French started putting a little thought into the appearance of their cars, they didn't sell well in Italy. That they were mechanically advanced with superb suspension, that they were reliable and easy to service cut no ice. The cars were ugly, and no one would buy them. Realizing this, the French left the design work to Italians in Turin, and immediately the cars began to sell.

Any Italian street is a fashion parade. At first glance the pavements appear to be peopled with extraordinarily good-looking creatures, causing visitors to remark on the physical beauty of the Italian race. Closer inspection shows a more ordinary range of attributes, but each Italian somehow accentuates their good features while disguising the bad. It is also true that their bearing, which screams confidence and self-esteem, helps to create the desired effect.

There is a sense of style in all aspects of daily life: in clothes, in accessories and in people's behaviour. Psychologists have suggested that our style of driving is a reflection of how we live our lives. Watch Italians driving through the traffic-choked streets of Rome for a living demonstration of panache. Everyone seems to know the exact length and width of their cars; tiny Fiats accelerate with their larger brothers, whole lines of cars move as one, instantly, as the lights go green. There is no dawdling, no hesitation. Vans whiz into spaces that seem large enough only for small cars. The omnipresent *Api*, the enclosed three wheelers built on a Vespa, manoeuvre deftly through traffic and over pavements. You can sense an almost tangible pride in the way the Italians throw their cars about, confident in their skill. There is a vicarious *frisson* as you watch the near misses, which rarely turn into close encounters. If the psychologists are right, then this is a mirror on the Italian way of life.

This is why car accidents generate so much heat among the protagonists. Somebody clearly screwed up, misread the situation, didn't fully appreciate their car's size. In short, somebody made a *brutta figura*, somebody lost face. No Italian would admit this readily, hence the roadside arguments. The self-perception of being in control, of confidence in their own abilities, is another facet of the drive for beauty. Elegance in behaviour is as important as elegance in dress. Anything that shakes this exposes an unpleasant ugliness, so must be avoided if possible.

Much of what Italians do during the day is a public statement. The bar you go to for coffee, the kind of cigarettes you smoke, what beer you drink – all are a carefully controlled expression of an Italian's public persona. Whereas in our valley beer used to be Peroni and only Peroni, nowadays you must be specific. If you ask simply for a beer, you will be served Stella Artois, or Heineken, or Carlsberg or anything but Peroni. Apart from the fact that a glass of imported draught will cost you more than a larger bottle of Peroni, and it is therefore in the publican's interest to serve it, it is becoming increasingly unfashionable to drink local beer. Drinking imported beer displays the drinker as cosmopolitan, worldly. Only the old and poor drink Peroni now, just as only the poor and the old smoke Italian Nazionali.

Actually, that needs clarifying. All cigarettes sold in Italy are manufactured by the state tobacco monopoly, Monital, so all cigarettes are Italian in that sense. However, it is the Italian-manufactured Winston, Marlboro and assorted foreign brands that are the fashionable smoke. Unlike in many other countries, smoking is still rife in Italy. I remember meeting some of the Italian cross-country skiing team practising in the Macchiarvana, near Pescaserroli. As we chatted they took their fags out and passed them round. As a smoker myself, I took encouragement from watching athletes do what I believed to be harmful.

Italians are less chauvinist than the French; they have always been prepared to absorb ideas and fashions from abroad. My guess is that they are so self-confident and pleased with their way of life that taking on ideas from others is no threat to their national or personal identity. On the crowded FM wave-band it is hard to find Italian music; American and English predominate. Because of the fascination with English-speaking music the young, particularly, are becoming fond of using English. 'Picnic', 'weekend', 'bungalow', 'cottage', 'stress' all regularly pepper conversations. Unfortunately for native English speakers, not all the words are used as they are in English. Because Italian puts the adjective after the noun rather than before it, some phrases get a little mangled. Apart from the standard forty-card deck, Italians also use the fifty-two-card pack that they call the poker deck. This includes two cards marked the 'Jolly Joker'. The joker is known universally as the 'Jolly'. 'Self-service' suffers the same fate, 'self' becoming the noun. Many petrol stations are boldly signed 'Self Area'. Golfing pullovers are known as 'golf's and jogging is inexplicably called 'footing'.

Language does not always travel well: the computer-games giant Sega sells defiantly in Italy with a brand name that means 'wank' in Italian. Still, Mitsubishi sells jeeps in Spain under the name Pajero which is slang for 'wanker', and for years General Motors sold a model to Spanish-speaking South America called the Nova – literally 'it doesn't go'. Irish Mist liqueur sells in Germany where mist means 'shit', so perhaps no one really cares.

The concern and the control that Italians exercise over their personal fashion statements extends to most of the family as well. Why are children so regimented? Why are teenagers so controlled? Why is calling an Italian male a cuckold such a pervasive and powerful insult? The answer lies in the need to control. Just as keeping oneself in control of one's life is important, so too are the extensions to that life. Unlike in England, there is no debate in Italy as to who is at fault if teenagers run wild. It is the parents, no question. There is no concept that society at large is to blame; the buck stops with the family. So it stands to reason that if you are going to get the blame for your offspring's bad behaviour, you must make some attempt to curb it.

This is why Caesar's wife was beyond reproach. To suggest otherwise is to imply that Caesar cannot control his wife – and if he can't control his wife, what hope is there for the empire? Why else should suggesting someone has an unhappy marriage be an insult? The insult factor in this hits an Italian male on his Achilles heel. It is because he believes that his wife's behaviour is somehow within his control that the suggestion of infidelity is so insulting. All Italian men believe that if you are a real stud, an Italian stallion, your wife will never look at another man since all her needs will be satisfied. The opposite also follows: if you are not sufficiently virile, with buckets of testosterone coursing through your veins, your wife will find a lover, hence the insult. What still puzzles me is that while this belief is held among men, the same men will boast endlessly of their conquests of other men's wives. Surely, I ask, if these women are available, if women all over Italy are eagerly awaiting an invitation to dalliance, then so too must your wife? This suggestion rarely meets with anything other than ridicule. 'My wife? You must be mad. She'd never do that to me.' Even this statement needs looking at. It suggests that a wife's infidelity is to spite or hurt the husband, not because she followed her desires in a moment of passion.

When I was a youth in the Gallinaro of the 1960s, modern ideas were still waiting in the wings. Young men and women got engaged as a prelude to marriage. It was just conceivable that an engagement could be broken, up to say six months, but after that a broken engagement left the girl with no further hope of marriage unless she emigrated. The reason for this is that a long engagement was understood to be a certain prelude to marriage. Therefore the two parties would almost certainly sleep together prior to the marriage, leaving the girl no longer a virgin, and thus no longer eligible for marriage. Logic played no part in these equations, that was just the way it was.

This system put enormous strains on people who discovered early in their engagement that it just wasn't working. It was so hard to back out that it was often easier to proceed. The kind of marriage that this produced made marital infidelity a foregone conclusion. This mentality is mostly history, but it is recent history, and it makes understanding modern parents a little simpler. There is a tendency for people who have undergone painful initiation rites to want others to go through them as well.

Still, even in the valley things are changing. There are young women who live their lives as they wish, with jobs and cars and little or no parental involvement. There are young, unmarried women who take their summer holidays with their boyfriends. What makes this worth reporting is not that it is accepted, but that it is still remarkable, still unusual enough to comment on. Of course it is not the young themselves who comment; for them it is entirely right and proper. It is the stalwarts of the old order, whose rearguard action is still being fought. That Italy has become secular enough in the past twenty years to pass referenda allowing divorce and abortion is remarkable, but it does not point to the disappearance of the *ancien régime*, only a temporary occlusion. For the moment the prevailing Euro-secularism holds sway in Italy, while the Catholic Church is battered by financial and sexual scandals, its mystique and authority eroded daily.

Twenty years ago the only access to ideas other than an exchange in the bar was from the one state television channel. Even until the 1970s this channel had peculiarities all of its own. For example, all the advertisements for the day were in one half-hour slot – at half past six, I think, called Carusello, and people actually watched it, as though it were a programme. In rural Italy ideas had been subject to little change, old shibboleths and taboos remained years after they had been broken elsewhere. There was a certainty about right and wrong, about behaviour and morality, that has now melted into the ether. In a way, it seems to me that the lack of certainty in all these things is what makes Italians so clubbable, so happy to be in a group. It is this urge for certainty that makes the slavish following of fashion so endemic.

No Italian fashion guru is going to say, 'This year everyone should make their own fashion statement; everyone should just go with their own colours and just be who you want to be.' How can you be confident and secure in your appearance if no one knows what is fashionable? This is the kernel of the insecurity that makes the fashion tyrants in Italy so powerful and rich. There is no history of personal fashion statements such as London experienced in the 1960s. Carnaby Street fashion got to Italy only after it had been made over by the Italian fashion houses. I remember at the time explaining that this missed the point, that the idea was to make your own fashion, not have it handed to you. It was a bit like selling the concept of igloos to the South American Guaranoto. Twenty-five years on, it's still a concept Italians have difficulty grasping. The old ideas die hard. Italian mums still iron creases into their sons' 501s.

Despite the repression of sexual behaviour by society and the Church, until recently there were still areas that had somehow been missed by the censors. Prostitution has never been a hidden, hush-hush trade in Italy, but always upfront and honest. It was and is accepted, if not as a necessity, then at least as an actuality that will always be there. Prostitutes are visible in Italy. They are on the motorway verges – at night with bonfires to keep themselves warm and to help to be seen; they work from home and in hotels. They are as prevalent as soft-core pornography, which is everywhere. The juxtaposition of strict Catholic morality and easily available sex for sale has always struck me as strange. Perhaps it is yet another example of that very Italian ability to live in the world not as we would wish it to be, but rather as it is. The same tolerance is shown to Catholic priests who fail in their vow of celibacy. Nobody finds it strange that this should happen, strange only that it hadn't happened sooner.

Italian women have close relationships with their sons. Areas that are taboo in some societies are not in Italy. Women will proudly point to their infant son's genitalia, to which the expected response is, 'Gosh, yes, really big, and such balls.' Even as sons grow older, their mothers continue a happy banter with them about their burgeoning sexuality. Although not used to it, I find that there is something comfortingly natural and uncomplicated in these exchanges. This kind of sexual banter comes as naturally to Italian women as breast feeding.

Since the days of the single television channel Italy has gone further down the road of deregulation than any other European state. It started with the FM radio band. It was deregulated in 1978, and anyone who wanted a licence to broadcast paid a £30 fee and was free to set up a radio station. Licences covered a low-power transmitter, which allowed a range of some 30 kilometres, so national networking was not a possibility. It did mean, however, that before long the Comino Valley was full of small radio stations hustling for advertising. Within a couple of years the good ones remained and the bad ones had failed from lack of advertising revenue.

So successful was this experiment in pleasing small interest groups and raising revenue for the state that the government took the plunge and decided to deregulate television as well. Apart from the state's three channels, each broadcasting area sells licences for fifty-six channels. In the early years every pressure group, every political party, every hopeful entrepreneur bought a licence, a top-floor flat and an aerial. Eight of my friends got together and started TV Sora. All of these new stations ran on second-hand equipment and relied on endless talking heads throughout the day and old videos run on endless loops throughout the night. They called it twenty-four hour broadcasting and it was very cheap. So cheap that questions formed in my mind as to the value for money given by national stations elsewhere in Europe with a maw ever greedy for increasing licence fees. Everyone needed advertising revenue to survive and to get that you needed viewers. Most of these embryonic stations stumbled upon the same sure-fire formula: sex.

Until these private stations came along, Italian game shows where housewives strip did not exist. This was the fare designed to wean the Italian viewing public from the state television service, the RAI. In those halcyon days of free-for-all broadcasting there was no nine o'clock watershed; sex was on TV from early morning till late at night. Oddly enough, no one seemed in a hurry to censor it. Whatever strictness there may be in Italy with regard to sexual morality, there is nothing Puritan about it, nor any urge to proselytize. My elderly relatives responded to the non-stop sex shows on the private stations by simply refusing to watch anything other than RAI.

The idea of sex as a hook was remarkably successful, and within three years several large television stations emerged. The original legislation had preserved national networking for the RAI. Private channels that eventually bought up licences for all of Italy could not network, that is, they could not show *I Love Lucy* in Milan at the same time as they did in Naples. Out of the mayhem of the first few years Silvio Berluscone built his empire.

Just as with radio, television stations with catchy titles like the Maoist and Trotskyist Progressive Television for the Proletariat and the Opus Dei Channel exhausted the resources of even their most fervent backers within the first couple of years. What remained was what the public wanted, but where did the sex go? Once the viewers had been won, the larger channels felt that going kosher would lend them more kudos, and the sex went out of it. If you really want to find it, you still can, but it is no longer the all-pervasive daily continuum it once was. *Colpo Grosso*, the quiz show where the contestants have to take all their clothes off, is still going. Going so well that now they use the topless dancers and the set in the Milan studio for German contestants and a German host, which is then exported as *Tutti Frutti* to a German satellite broadcasting channel. A good example of pan-European co-operation.

For the most part Italian men and women do not have competitive relationships. There is an easy understanding between the sexes of their different roles. The women decide on all matters pertaining to the home, friends and children, while the men decide what car to buy. Some men even choose their own clothes. In my teens I was struck by how easy and comfortable relationships with Italian girls were. Once I had grasped the fact that sex was not available prior to a long engagement and simply enjoyed the relationship without looking for sexual gratification, I found these relationships to be infinitely more satisfying than many in England or

Ireland where sex figured prominently. There is a lot less trench warfare between the sexes and a good deal of openness.

My mother has a great friend from her school days who lives in Aversa, about half-way between Gallinaro and Naples. Romilda, a beautiful black-haired lady, has three gorgeous daughters, all roughly my age. During those teenage years I spent a lot of time in Aversa, and as soon as I had a driving licence I drove my Fiat 500 there as often as I could. For once it was not testosterone driving me, but rather a chance to talk to girls as an equal, with few if any barriers between us. It was while I was staying in Aversa one year with Mimma, Giovanna and Valeria that I made a discovery. The girls were having a party and that night I was awestruck at the gathering. All the boys and all the girls seemed so amazingly sophisticated, well-dressed, confident, while I felt distressingly dull. For what seemed like an eternity I found reasons to be in the kitchen, the bathroom, anywhere but where I would have to confront these beautiful people. The girls' father, Rafaele, was a competent pianist and had a good voice. He began playing Neapolitan songs wonderfully, but this was the era of the Rolling Stones and the Beatles. In desperation he singled me out.

'Paolo, you can play that Americano "hippy-hippy yay", can't you?'

I knew what he meant by this curious phrase and said I could. I played. Suddenly the mask of sophistication that surrounded me on all sides became transparent. I could see young faces no different from I those I would find in England or Ireland and my discomfort vanished. The simple truth that people are much the same no matter how they appear was a revelation to me that night. I found myself fêted and appreciated by the very creatures who had seemed so remote, so unattainable. Since that night that peculiarly Italian ability to create anxiety in less beautiful mortals no longer affects me. I now see their beauty not as a threat – indeed it was never intended to be so – but rather as a part of what makes Italy so interesting and exciting.

# 12

# *The Italian Larder*

By now it must be abundantly clear that food figures largely in my life, and in that of the Comino Valley. What follows is foodie indulgence: a guide for basic gastronomy Lazio-style.

To eat Italian food on a daily basis you need a *cantina*, or larder, stocked with some basic ingredients: *prosciutto, salsicce*, both fresh and preserved in oil, curd cheese, herbs either dry or in oil, pasta, and several kinds of sauce. I know of no books on Italian cooking that tell you how to make these staples, so here is a quick tour.

The main principle is that whatever keeps should be made in quantity at one time and then stored for later use. It saves time in the long run and you eat better. The other point to remember is that there are no short cuts; the preparation is labour-intensive and takes time, but if you care about how you eat, it's worth it.

In the Comino Valley, as elsewhere in Italy, the yearly cycle starts in the winter when the pig is killed. It's done in winter because the process of salt-curing works better when the weather is cool and dry. The two back legs become *prosciutto*, the sides are cured rather like bacon – *pancetta* – and, apart from what little is eaten fresh, the rest becomes sausages. Should you wish to try it, the process is easy enough. Buy the biggest haunch of fresh pork you can find: 7 kilos would be the minimum, over 9 is better. Lay the leg on a bed of coarse salt in a tray that allows the liquid pickle to drain out. Now cover the top of the leg with salt, working it well into the shank end and into the crevices around the hip bone. Leave it there for twice as many days as it weighs in kilos, checking it occasionally to ensure it remains covered in salt. When the time is up, wash it clean of salt and dry it thoroughly. Now hang it up in a cool and airy place and watch it carefully. Any sign of mould, or any hint of rot around the hip bone must be treated immediately with fine salt, worked into the crevices. After ten days to a fortnight it should have a dry exterior; all drips should have stopped. What is happening is that the salt is drawing the moisture out of the meat. The drier and airier the environment the faster this happens.

At this point you can try one of two techniques for the next stage. I prefer to wipe the exposed flesh with olive oil and then pat it with powdered chilli, which will give the ham a red colour, a lovely smell and will eventually flavour the *prosciutto*. Try to avoid getting the chilli powder on the skin – it spoils the look of it. If you wish, rub olive oil into the skin, which will, over time, give it a golden colour. Now hang it up again and wait. How long you wait depends on your patience, but don't start cutting into it until it has lost at least a third of its original weight. This will usually take a minimum of seven to nine months, so watch it carefully as the summer comes for signs of rot or mould. More salt is the cure.

The other technique to use when the ham is surface dry is to make a paste of flour, water and salt and spread this over the exposed meat fairly thinly. Like the chilli powder, this has the effect of discouraging the attention of flies, as well as improving the look of the ham. If by chance you should leave your *prosciutto* too long and it becomes as hard as iron, don't despair. Leave it to soak in a mixture of half-wine, half-water and it will become delicious again.

Sausages – *salsicce* – are a staple. They turn up in many

dishes and are a snack on their own. Shoulder of pork has about the right mix of lean meat to fat for sausages – to cure properly they need a minimum of one third fat content. To start off with 5 kilos is enough, but if you're feeling energetic, 10 kilos makes a lot of sausages. The meat should be cut into small cubes, preferably by hand. Machine chopping tends to heat the meat and you'll end up with black sausages; the same holds true of mincing. Take a large mixing bowl and cover the bottom about 3 centimetres deep with the chopped pork. Sprinkle this well with salt, coarsely ground black pepper and chilli powder. A pinch of saltpetre helps the preserving but is not essential. Now add another layer of meat and repeat the salt, pepper and chilli. Continue until you have used all the pork and then mix it all together thoroughly.

Next you will need casings for the sausages. They come in two kinds, natural and artificial. Either will do, but you need casings that will fill to at least 4 centimetres in diameter without bursting. Most butchers are happy to sell them. Now you must be ingenious. There are, of course, machines that fill sausages, but they are hardly standard kitchen appliances. You need a funnel with a long, wide spout, at least 2 centimetres in diameter. Tie a knot in one end of the casing and work the rest over the spout, like fitting a prophylactic, until the knot is at the end of the spout. If the casing is salted and dry, soak it and run warm water through it first. Now you must find a way to force the meat down the spout. A glass of red wine added to the pork will make it easier to push into the casing, but the sausages will take longer to cure because of the added liquid. The simplest device for pushing the pork into the casing, but the hardest work, is a piping bag with a nozzle wide enough to take the funnel. Squeeze the bag, or use a rod to plunge the funnel and the casing will slowly come off the spout as it fills with meat. It is important to make sure that the casing is well filled and taut; keep a little pressure on it to make sure it doesn't slide off the spout too quickly, leaving you with half-filled sausage. Eventually you will end up with a tube 1.5 metres long stuffed with pork.

Over the years I have successfully used an old Spong mincer with the blades removed and my funnel attached to the front with a jubilee clip. I have also used the device for squeezing silicon out of tubes, but best of all is any electrically powered screw such as on a mincer, modified to hold the funnel.

If you get this far, you will now have a long sausage. Gently tighten a length of string about 10 centimetres from one end, making your first sausage in the line. Loop the string further along and make a second sausage, continuing until you reach the other end. Take your string of *salsicce* and hang them up as with the *prosciutto*, where it is cool and dry. Note their weight, and when they weigh half of their original weight, pack them tightly into storage jars and cover them completely with olive oil. If you don't do this, the *salsicce* will continue to shrink and will eventually become so hard that they will be inedible. In a jar of oil they will theoretically keep for ever; the trouble is that they taste so good, they go in no time. Slice them thinly with a diagonal cut to get larger slices and eat them on bread.

Sausages made like this don't have to be left to cure. Take a couple after a day or two and slice them lengthways. Cook them on a griddle iron for a real treat, or better still on wood embers. You can put them into your *sugo* while it cooks to add flavour. Their uses are endless. They can be made all year long if they are going to be cooked, but if they are for curing and storing, winter is the best time.

There is a wonderful pasta dish that you can make using the *salsicce*, either fresh or cured. It is called *spaghetti alla carbonara*. Traditionally this was made by charcoal burners, who spent the summers in the high mountains cutting wood and making charcoal, returning in the autumn with their produce. Because they would normally have only one heat source – an open fire – and probably only one pot for boiling the pasta, this dish was popular, since it could be made with these limited resources. I have seen many recipes for this dish that include butter and cream, but they are gentrified versions of the original plain, delicious, rustic fare. The basic mountain recipe is this: boil the spaghetti, when it is cooked drain it, leaving it in the pot. Break four eggs per half kilo of pasta and drop them in, add some olive oil and some chopped *salsicce*. Stir well and eat.

I have always been hesitant to try to improve on this simple dish, but without over-elaborating it you can try this. While the spaghetti cooks let some chopped, fresh *salsicce* simmer slowly in a frying pan with plenty of olive oil and, if cholesterol is not a problem, some pieces of fat from the *prosciutto*. Again, for half a kilo of pasta, take four egg yolks, discarding the whites. Whisk these well with half an eggshell of water and grate fresh Parmesan into it. If the cheese is very dry the mixture will thicken – thin it down again with another drop of water. Add freshly ground black pepper and whisk some more. When the pasta is cooked drain it and return it to the pot. Pour in the *salsicce* and oil first and stir well. Now add the eggs, stirring quickly. If you have done this with speed, the residual heat of the pasta will cook the eggs and there is no need for further heat. Don't let the egg cook until it sets; it should coat the pasta like cream. It is worth the effort of making *salsicce* for this alone.

This dish embodies the philosophy of food in the south of Italy. Although much of what is prepared is labour-intensive, it is very rarely complex. What is appreciated is the quality of the raw ingredients, and the skilful use of flavour. Mixed herbs are not to be found in little jars in Italian supermarkets – Italians like flavours that are clearly defined. Using too many flavours is like mixing too many colours together –

you get muddy brown. The best example of the careful use of flavours is *gremolata*, the traditional accompaniment to *osso buco*. Combine chopped parsley, garlic and grated lemon rind and you end up with a taste that is greater than its parts – it makes a new flavour entirely, just as a painter mixing blue and yellow makes a new colour.

Now that the larder contains cured pork ready for use, we need some cheese. The only cheese that can be made at home with pasteurized milk is soft curd cheese, which makes a good substitute for *ricotta*. You can make a small amount with 4 litres of milk, which will yield about 500 grammes of cheese, depending on the habits of your dairy. Warm the milk slowly to 32 degrees centigrade, take it off the heat and then stir in rennet. This can be bought in chemists, and usually one tablespoon of rennet per litre of milk is recommended. In about half an hour the milk will set into curd. Leave it overnight; then the next day drain off the whey and break up the curd. Ladle it into a piece of linen or cheesecloth and tie it tightly, leaving it to drain for another hour. Untie it, and work 50 grammes of salt into the curds, adding if you wish some herbs for flavouring. *Ricotta* should be left unflavoured for use in cooking and, although this is not *ricotta*, it will be closer to it if it is simply salted and not flavoured. When it's salted, tie it up again and leave it. You can eat it fresh, but you can also leave it to mature for a month or more if you brush the outside of the cheese with salted water regularly. If you have little wicker baskets, put the curds in those instead of tying them up in cloth. In baskets the cheese should be turned every two days.

If you can get your hands on fresh, unpasteurized milk, you can make some real cheese, like *mozzarella*. Bring 10 litres of milk up to 30 degrees centigrade. Remove from the heat, add the rennet and cover. Cut the curds when they are set, and bring the curds and whey back up to 30 degrees. Cover and put somewhere warm. Now you have to be dedicated. Wait half a day, then start to test your curds for pitching. As the curds sit in the whey they become increasingly acid: this is pitching. Take a small piece of curd on a fork and dip it into boiling water. If when you take it out you can make it go stringy, it's ready. If not, leave it and test every three hours until it is.

When the curds are pitched, pour off the whey and put small amounts of the curd into really hot water. Work the curds and slowly you can make small balls of cheese by rolling the stringy bits around themselves. Make balls about the size of a lemon, and put them into salted water for an hour. Now you can eat your *mozzarella*.

If you press your curds into moulds rather than immersing them in hot water, you will have *caciotta*. If you turn the cheese every two days and paint the outside with salted water regularly, after a month, your cheese will be hard enough to use for grating.

To be really clever, take the whey that you poured off the curds and add either lemon juice or vinegar. Slowly heat this to near boiling point. Milk solids will begin to precipitate. When cool, pour through very fine muslin or cheese-cloth and you have real *ricotta*, which, incidentally, means re-cooked.

There are two types of pasta: fresh and dried. The dry pasta is the one in every shop; it keeps for ages so there is no harm in having the larder stocked with a variety of shapes. Italians are very fussy about what shapes go with what sauce and there is sense in this. Every sauce has different properties when it comes to coating the pasta; for example, thick sauces do not work well on the cut pasta such as *penne* or *rigatoni*, since the insides of the tubes don't get covered. You end up eating a high proportion of pasta to sauce. Thick sauces that contain little oil or butter work best on *fusilli* or *spaghetti*, where the surface area is large in proportion to the volume. These are not hard and fast rules, but are worth observing.

Fresh pasta does not keep for long, so it is usually made for immediate consumption. It makes a change from the other and is not hard to make – it is only flour and eggs. Any white wheat flour will do, but the best results come from using hard durum wheat flour, type oo. Four eggs to half a kilo of flour is normal; depending on the size of the eggs, you may need to

add a little water or more flour to make a stiff dough. Work it long and hard and then roll it out into thin sheets. Use a knife to cut it either into thin strips, *tagliatelle*, or into pieces about 15 by 5 centimetres, *lasagne*. Fresh pasta like this cooks quickly – about four or five minutes.

You can make more than you intend to eat right away. If you hang your *tagliatelle* over a line it will dry quickly and keep for a week or so with no problems. *Lasagne* will need plenty of work surfaces where you can lay out the pieces on floured boards or trays until they are dry. After that they can be packed loosely into boxes until they are needed. To make a good *lasagna* cook the pasta first, before you tray it up. If you don't, all the starch remains in the pasta instead of in the cooking water and your *lasagna* will be a stodgy lump.

On occasions *gnocchi* make a change from pasta. They are made from potato and flour. The secret for good, delicate *gnocchi*, as opposed to hard little bullets, is using as little flour as possible. The principle is straightforward: stiffen mashed potato with flour to make a firm dough. The less water the boiled potatoes contain, the less flour you need to make a stiff paste. Waxy potatoes work better than floury ones; steaming works better than boiling.

As a rough guide, the ratio of potato to flour should be four to one, that is, for a kilo of potatoes you'll need about 250 grammes of flour. Mix this together with two eggs and a knob of butter and roll it out into pieces the thickness of a finger. Cut the roll into lengths of about 2 cm and give each piece a squeeze in the middle with your forefinger and thumb. Put them one at a time into simmering, salted water and remove them with a perforated spoon when they float to the top. Treat them as pasta, but ideally serve with a strong, full-bodied sauce, such as a meat *sugo*.

The other farinaceous dish eaten in Italy is *polenta*, boiled maize meal. Depending on how thick you want the final product to be, take one measure of maize semolina and add between two-and-a-half and three measures of water. A mug of semolina makes enough for six smallish portions. Put the maize into a pan of boiling water and start stirring. Add three teaspoonfuls of salt. As you keep stirring the *polenta* will begin to thicken, making disgusting noises as it does so. Turn the heat low and let it make plopping sounds, stirring occasionally. When it is thick enough to stand the spoon in it, turn off the heat. There are many recipes to be found for this, but the best is simple. Have prepared a good tomato sauce with plenty of olive oil in it, in which you have cooked some *salsicce*. Spread the polenta out in a flat container, about a centimetre thick. Cover it with sauce and sausages. If you have any left over, cut it into squares and fry it in oil the next day – nearly as good as cold pasta.

Preserving food in a jar of oil is an ancient tradition. It keeps your *salsicce* until they are devoured, but is excellent for many other uses. If you grow basil, drying it loses a lot of flavour. Pack the leaves well down into a jar and cover them with oil, taking care to get air bubbles out. Not only will the flavour keep better, but you'll have a jar of basil-flavoured oil as well. This property of olive oil can be put to use with chilli peppers. Many Italian recipes need a touch of chilli and gauging the amount to use is never easy. A simple solution is to break dried chillis into a jar, and cover them plus that height again with oil. After four or five weeks the oil will be red and fiery. Now you can dose yourself by the teaspoon and the fire of the chillis is easier to disperse throughout the sauce.

For the quickest of meals try *spaghetti all' aglio e olio* – the *pasto del cornuto*. While the spaghetti cooks, warm some olive oil in a pan with crushed or sliced garlic. Do not let the garlic brown, as this makes it indigestible. Add one or two teaspoonfuls of chilli oil and when the spaghetti is cooked strain the oil and pour it over the pasta. There is nothing simpler, and it is delicious.

When the glut of tomatoes comes in summer they are traditionally boiled, skinned and put into preserving jars. They can then be used throughout the following year for tomato sauces. If there are three or four days of strong sun, you can try sun-dried tomatoes. I have managed on occasion in Ireland, so it should be possible anywhere in Europe. Take the tomatoes and slice them lengthways, if possible leaving the skin on one side intact, so that they open like a book. Put the tomatoes on a board, so that in the event of a shower they can be moved under cover quickly. Salt the exposed flesh well, and let the sun do its work. When they look like shrivelled bats' wings, they are ready. Once again, preserve them in oil or they'll become drier and drier.

Some of the best food in Italy is cooked on the fire embers. This is not the same as using a barbecue, requiring a little more care. Any wood will do, but a mixture of dry and green is best. Wood such as apple or pear imparts a lovely flavour, as do beech and oak. Avoid tarry woods like conifers. Stack the wood high, like a tower built of matches. Let it blaze well before knocking it down and spreading it out. Now put a trivet or something similar over the fire, so that your grid will be no more than 2 or 3 centimetres above the fire. Wood embers emit considerably less heat than charcoal, so the food must be close to the fire. You also have less time to cook with wood embers, so get everything on at the same time. Pork chops work very well cooked like this, as do thin slices of beef – fillet or rump steak. Keep a jug of water handy to sprinkle on any flames caused by burning fat; there should be only glowing embers, no flame. When the meat is cooked, cut some slices of bread and rub both sides with oil and a clove of garlic. Brown both sides over the embers and you have *bruschetta*. Use the dying embers to roast sweet peppers. Put them directly on the embers, turning them until all parts are literally black. Wash them under running water and the black comes off, exposing perfectly cooked pepper beneath. Slice them into thin strips, add a little crushed garlic and plenty of oil, then put them in the fridge for a day. You may never eat peppers any other way again.

Autumn is the time for gathering mushrooms. Common and good varieties include ceps, field and horse mushrooms, parasols and shaggy ink-caps. Ceps can be dried by slicing them and putting them on newspaper somewhere warm, such as over an Aga, keeping each slice separate from the others. They can be reconstituted in water later, when they are needed. The other kinds can be cooked and then frozen. The best mushroom sauce for pasta that I know needs 450 grammes of fresh mushrooms diced very small. A food processor will do it faster and finer. Cook the finely diced mushrooms in a frying pan with a little olive oil. Put a lid on the pan and stir occasionally, keeping the heat low. After half an hour remove the lid and add a little cream, stirring well. Now grate 125 grammes of *caciotta* or white cheddar into the pan, stirring constantly. Keep the heat low or the cheese will burn. If the sauce becomes thick, add more cream. Salt it very well and add some black pepper. This is enough sauce for a half-kilo packet of pasta. The best pasta for this is *fusilli*, a spiral shape with plenty of surface area.

Finally, the larder contains wine and liqueurs. Making wine is beyond the scope of this book, but some liqueurs are easy to make and very good. Ideally to make a liqueur you need pure alcohol. In France, Italy and Spain it can be bought in any supermarket by the litre. If you have no access to some, you can get by with the strongest, least flavoured vodka that you can find. If you can begin with alcohol, take half a litre of water and warm it, dissolving 200 grammes of sugar into it. When it has cooled, pour it into a 2-litre preserving jar and add half a litre of alcohol. You now have a mixture of 50 per cent alcohol by volume. If this is stronger than you would like (whisky is 40 per cent), just add water.

To get to this point with vodka, warm it as little as possible (so as not to evaporate the alcohol) and dissolve 200 grammes of sugar per litre into it. An ordinary bottle of 75 centilitres will need 150 grammes of sugar.

With the liquid in the jar, take the finest orange that you can find, perfumed, ripe and without blemish. Thread string or wool through the middle of the orange. Now, holding both ends of the string, lower the orange into the preserving jar until it is a centimetre or so above the liquid. It is important that the orange is not in contact with the liquid. When it is in position, keep holding the string and close the lid of the jar, trapping the string and leaving the orange suspended. Put the jar away for three weeks and then open it, remembering not to let the orange fall. You will be met with the smell of Cointreau and a taste – if you used pure alcohol – indistinguishable from it.

Lastly, to finish an Italian meal there is nothing quite like a digestive liqueur. In the Comino Valley this is *nocino*, made from walnuts. You need to pick unripe nuts in June or July when they are still soft enough to slice with a knife. Slice through both the green outer covering and the nut, cutting each one into four. Chop enough to loosely fill a 2-litre preserving jar, and pour a litre of alcohol into it. Seal it and wait eight weeks. Pour the alcohol, which will now be dark brown, into another jar with one vanilla pod and leave it for another month. Now add a litre of water in which you have dissolved 400 grammes of sugar, including as part of the litre a small cup of percolated black coffee as an optional extra. Now is the time to bottle it. You can drink it at this stage, but it will improve dramatically with time, mellowing into a fine *digestivo*.

The basic recipe for any liqueur is a litre of 50 per cent alcohol by volume, 200 grammes of sugar and your choice of flavour. Graziano's wild strawberry liqueur is made just like the *nocino*; steep the berries in alcohol for two months.

A well-stocked larder not only lets you eat well, it permits

impromptu hospitality, something Italians love. It also satisfies the desire in Italians to order their world, to *sistemare*. In the Comino Valley it has historical echoes: it is a bulwark keeping the wolf from the door, a daily reminder that poverty and *miseria* are a thing of the past.

# 13

# *Pyrotechnics and Drama*

It's probably true that all rural, agricultural societies have markets. They serve the dual purpose of getting produce to a prospective buyer while fulfilling a social role, providing a time, a place and a reason for isolated individuals to come together. Of the twelve towns in the Comino Valley, seven have weekly markets. The largest one is in Atina and is held every Monday.

Markets start early in Italy; the traders arrive before six to set up their stalls and shortly after people begin to arrive. I have this information second-hand, since I have never made it before ten. The drive to Atina is one to take with care – the road snakes up from the valley floor forming a series of hair-pin bends as it climbs. Sections of the road are lined with the remnants of the pre-Roman walls that once surrounded the citadel. As the road climbs it passes remains of Roman walls, more recent than the Samnite ones, part brick and part stone. Still further, it goes past one of the medieval gates, through which some of the later Roman buildings can be seen. From here on the road is hard to negotiate on market-day. Cars line both sides of the road, while people meander slowly in the middle of the street oblivious to traffic. At the top of the hill is the nearest thing Atina has to a flat space. In front of the impressive late-medieval gate is a wide sloping area, which, combined with the road itself, is where the stalls are laid out.

This extra-mural part of the market sells hardware, shoes, clothes, leather goods, bootleg tapes and household goods. Anyone not speaking Italian, or unused to the ways of the souk, should either not buy here, or be prepared to spend over the odds. Haggling is integral to the event: it is expected. No stalls carry prices except for a couple of the shoe stalls – you have to ask. The trader then appraises you and, using all the skills he has acquired over a lifetime, quotes a price that he feels you might just be prepared to accept. How much less than this you eventually arrive at is a function of how long you are prepared to argue, how keen the trader is to sell, and how well you can negotiate. The Italian for 'shop' incidentally is *negozio*, hence 'negotiate'. There is little more annoying than haggling for ten minutes reducing the asking price to half, and then next day finding the same object in a supermarket for less. If you have time to spare, though, it's fun to haggle and it is a genuinely Italian pleasure to shop at the market.

There is a very visible hierarchy of traders. At the top of the tree are flashy new vans that open out like a concertina, becoming a high-tech shop. Then there are the dusty old diesels whose contents are emptied on to trestles with canvas awnings to protect the goods and traders from sun or rain. There are Moroccans, whose wares are on converted prams, constantly moving, because to stop and trade requires a payment to the *comune* of Atina. Just at the arch of the main town gate there is an old lady who sells wickerwork. She sits on a chair, with her produce arrayed around her feet. The little baskets that she sells are made specifically as cheese moulds. Fresh *ricotta* or curd cheese is put into these baskets to set, giving it the traditional pattern on the surface. Until recently, the toy stalls sold ingenious Eastern-European tin toys with sharp edges, mostly clockwork, of the kind that could be found in Britain in the 1930s.

Inside the gate, in the old town centre, are the fruit and

vegetable stalls, which surround the ducal palace, a fine building dating from the fifteenth century. There is a cornucopia of produce here which tempts by its very abundance. And every year my wife vows that she will never again get ripped-off at the market. The scams are as varied as they are ingenious. Scales, the old hand-held lever variety, are manipulated as though by magic; carefully chosen produce is switched under your nose for lesser quality as it is bagged; change needs to be checked punctiliously. So why do we bother? Because it's fun to pit your wits against the traders, because it's street theatre, because if you are careful, this is the best produce available. It's colourful and noisy, the smells are mesmerizing and it's a place to see and be seen. When you tire of the haggle, the cafés have welcoming tables set outside so you can drink a reviving *espresso* while watching the unfolding drama of market day.

The best bargains to be had in Italian markets are shoes and leather goods. For real quantity and variety Atina market pales into insignificance compared to Sora or Cassino. There are literally hundreds of shoe stalls in these two markets. What makes the bargains so good is once again the slavish following of fashion. Every year the big shoe manufacturers of the north sell off what remains of last year's fashion, at what must be a pittance, since the stall-holders charge so little. Top-quality men's shoes cost around 50,000 lire, about £25, after a little discussion, and women's shoes go for much less. Unfortunately there is no point in finding a style you like and asking, 'Have you got this in a 37?' If it's not on display, they haven't. People with either tiny or huge feet get the best bargains, as obviously shoes in these sizes are the hardest to sell.

Markets are where you can find spurious leather goods, marked Armani or Valentino, but almost certainly made in Naples. Like Far-Eastern Rolex copies, they have a certain cachet and, at less than a tenth of shop prices, are worth examining. The local markets are the only place that you can get fresh fish and this is the reason that many women go in the first place.

Love of drama is something that the visitor to Italy notices almost at once. Even simple events can be, and are, invested with a dramatic content that to a non-Italian can seem wildly out of proportion with what happened. A child falling and grazing a knee can result in huge numbers of adults stopping whatever they were doing and rushing to the scene. Everyone joins in the furore, there is a speaking part for everyone. 'Do we need an ambulance? Shall I call a doctor? There's a chemist round the corner, shall I get a bandage?' Briefly, a sobbing child sits centre-stage surrounded by a cacophony of voice. Amongst the many things the child learns during these moments is that there is an ever-evolving drama out there in which he has a part. Life is for the playing. Do Italian women really find it easier to lower a basket on a rope from a first-floor window to calling traders than to go downstairs? By the time a basket has done all the journeys needed to complete a transaction, it surely represents more work, more ergs expended. And yet, where is the drama in going downstairs?

Like markets, the *festa* provides for Italians a backdrop, a theatrical set against which the dramas of daily life can be played out. In the Comino Valley alone there are fifty-seven religious *feste* a year, many of them running for two or three days. In less prosperous times that was all there was, but these days more events have been added. According to my official gazetteer of events, there were 204 public events in all. As well as the *feste* there are film festivals, music festivals, art festivals, theatre festivals, competitions involving swimming, running, cycling, orienteering and hang-gliding, to name but a few. A recent addition to all of this has been the *sagra*, which basically means feast in the food sense. Over the course of the year there is a *sagra* of beans, watermelons, bread, figs, polenta, omelettes and wild boar – all this without leaving the valley.

Italians love to dress up and participate, or to dress up and watch. They feel anxious if there is an event in which they could be taking a part but are not. There is an urge to be involved, to be seen to be there, to play one's part in the drama. A *festa* is an excuse to put on one's finery, to meet up with the gang and get out into the fray. I am no longer surprised at how few books can be found in the average Italian house; they really don't have time to read when there is so much socializing going on. There seems to be a prevalent belief that being on your own is a sorry state in which to find yourself. If I stay in the house for an evening, there is always someone calling to find out whether we are coming out, or proffering an invitation to an event to entice us. Solitary is not the Italian way.

The *festa* is the only excuse left for women to put on their traditional costumes. Many of these have been handed down over the generations, and some have magnificent lace and needlework. Each town in the Comino Valley had its own variation of the regional costume. It was possible to tell at a glance from which town a girl came simply by looking at the costume. The basic design is a pleated black skirt with up to ten petticoats beneath, a heavily embroidered white blouse, a black lace shawl and a lace head-covering. Gallinaro's peculiarity was a flat, square board inside the head-covering, over which the lace hung, framing the face. In times gone by the costume was one way that a young girl could impress a prospective husband with the quality of her needlework.

The men's costume is less ornate: black breeches, black waistcoat and a white shirt topped with a red bandanna. On their feet they wear *cioce*, Frosinone's traditional footwear. The feet and calves are bound in white cotton, and a leather sole is strapped to the foot, the thongs criss-crossing the calf,

up to the knee. These *cioce* are what has given the province of Frosinone its sobriquet of Ciociaria.

These costumes have now become little more than theatrical accessories – less attention is paid to local nuances and they are worn only to cut a *bella figura* at a *festa*.

On 11 August Gallinaro celebrates the feast of its patron saint, San Gerardo. Preparations start about a week beforehand as the team arrives to erect the festival lights. On large lattice-work arches patterns of small lights are attached, with a cavalier disdain for safety. Fencing-wire is stapled to the lattice in paired lines connected to the grid, one positive, one negative. The lights are simply strapped across the pair. The fact that no one gets electrocuted must be thanks to the protection of San Gerardo. These arches of lights are placed along the main road every ten metres or so, and are very pretty at night.

On 9 August the stalls begin to arrive, some the same as you can find in the market, but some specifically tailored for *feste*. The piazza outside the Sanctuary slowly fills with fairground amusements and both sides of the road are filled with *bancarelle*, market stalls, up to the top of the hill. *Festa* favourites include stalls selling roast nuts and *porchetta*, suckling pig boned and roasted whole. Slices of piglet are served on fresh bread to be eaten at an amble. Other food stalls provide the unlikely delicacy of calf's head, boiled until soft enough to slice. Apart from food, a perennial favourite is the stall selling minute cap-guns that deliver a quite disproportionate report, which appeal to the Italians' delight in noise. Every year there is a toy which catches the imagination of the children. Last year it was a plastic slinky, in a variety of gaudy colours, which dangled from the hands of most of the small children.

The noise is nearly overwhelming: the stalls blare music from cheap speakers, the stall-holders cry their wares, the cap-guns bang. To complete the discord, a prerequisite of any *festa* is the band, which plays at random times throughout the day. The musicians, uniformed and shuffling, wander the streets, a bored look on their faces and a wilful individuality in their playing. They seem to save their worst-rehearsed numbers for the start of the singing during the procession – for as long as I can remember the band has always accompanied the hymn to San Gerardo with an entirely different melody.

The real crowds arrive in the evening for the music and fireworks. Every night of the *festa* there is music in the Piazza Santa Maria. It is a varied programme, reflecting the Italians' catholic taste in music. There is always a night with a rock band, one with Neapolitan music and one with a dance orchestra.

My friend Graziano is a big, bearded Communist – well, nowadays he's a member of the Democratic Left. He became

a councillor at the last local election and was given the job of administrator in charge of tourism and culture. Organizing the entertainment for the *festa* is his job. Because of his political affiliation, in 1991 he was able to get, through the Chinese Embassy in Rome, a folklore troupe from Tsinan in

Shantung province to come to Gallinaro. Since they were travelling to the valley anyway, the committee of the Atina Folklore Festival booked them as well, immediately prior to our *festa*. I went with Graziano to meet the Chinese in a hotel in Atina. We were met by the artistic director, the musical director and a sour-faced lady of indeterminate age who was introduced as the interpreter. It transpired that she spoke no Italian at all, only English – and that was pretty ropey. Still, we organized the times and got a list of what they needed by way of PA and props. They would also need to be fed after the show, all forty of them.

As we drove back to Gallinaro we considered how and what to feed them. I suggested some kind of rice dish, but Graziano thought they must be sick of rice. We went to see Alberto, the mayor. He promptly decided that the only solution was, hang the expense, take them to a restaurant. There are two good restaurants in Gallinaro, one in the Hotel Tramps, the other Chez Vital. Vitale is a gifted chef even by Italian standards. We phoned both of these to get a rough idea of cost – both of them were well beyond the budget. We went to see Desiderio, who has the *pizzeria* on the road leading to the Chapel of the Baby Jesus. He promised us good wine, beer and a three-course meal that was well within the budget, so we booked.

The performance by the Chinese the next evening was without a doubt the most impressive show that I have seen anywhere for a long time. There were dainty ballerinas of extraordinary elegance, jugglers, conjurors, musicians who played a bewildering variety of instruments, and stunning costumes. The performance was world class, and it occurred to me that this troupe must be wondering precisely what their political masters were doing sending them to a small, hill-top village in the remote mountains of Italy.

After the show we led their bus to Desiderio's, where he had laid tables outside overlooking the western end of the valley. I was seated between the sour-faced interpreter and the two directors; Graziano was at another table surrounded by six beautiful ballerinas. As a special treat Desiderio had laid each place with some *prosciutto*, as an *antipasto* – a little extra to thank the performers. I beamed at the assembled company as they began to eat. Suddenly all the Chinese were gagging inelegantly and spitting out the ham. The interpreter explained that they don't eat raw pork in China. I tried to explain that it was not raw, to no avail: the meal was in danger of becoming a serious loss of face. No one seemed to be touching the wine either. I was beginning to panic. The rotund and jovial artistic director pointed to his glass and said the only words of Engrish that he knew: 'Coca Cora.' Within minutes all was well, smiles returned, the ham was forgotten and the tables resounded with happy laughter. No wonder this liquid has conquered the world.

Despite immense goodwill, conversation was difficult. The interpreter had difficulty understanding me, while her attempts at English were as easy to decipher as an Inca quipu. Alberto, the mayor, arrived towards the end of the meal and after the introductions the artistic director got up to speak. It was clearly a formal address, thanking the mayor for the invitation to the *festa*, but was interspersed with loud belches. This seemed to have no effect on the Chinese, for whom it must be acceptable etiquette, but the effect on the Italians was dreadful to behold. They couldn't stop giggling. The Chinese were clearly perplexed as to the reason for this and the artistic director bravely continued, belching all the while. This potentially embarrassing moment thankfully passed and there followed an exchange of gifts. We sat over coffee, continuing our efforts to communicate.

'Are you all Communists?' I was asked, with a finger pointing at Graziano.

'No, no. The mayor' – I pointed to him – 'is a Socialist, so

is our administration. That town over there' – more gestures
– 'is Christian Democrat. That one is Communist.'

I watched as incomprehension gradually spread over the
interpreter's pinched face.

'This one Socialist. That one Democrat. Each town different, yes?'

No. I gave up. I did notice, however, that although the
two directors were leaning forwards, trying to glean the gist
of what I had said, the lady refused to translate. I decided that
she was no interpreter, given her lack of ability, but a
member of the political police, determined that travel should
not broaden the minds of her charges.

Even in a town as small as Gallinaro large sums of money
are spent on the *festa*. At the moment the state provides
money, so does the region, the *comune* itself, and the individual
donations from the villagers top that up. Some £30,000 is
spent on bands, evening entertainment and fireworks. With
this kind of money to spend, a *festa* committee can afford
some good entertainers, even national stars. A large proportion of the money goes up in smoke. No *festa* is complete
without the *pirotecnici*, the fireworks. They pepper the day
with bangs, but at night the spectacular displays come into
their own. No celebration would be complete without the
noise, smell and visual delights of the fireworks.

An average display for a small village like ours lasts about
twenty minutes. There are no pauses, just a continuous bar-
rage of light and sound in the sky. Some of the latest
additions to the art of pyrotechnics are wonderful. There is a
new firework that goes very high, explodes with a loud bang,
and slowly becomes a huge blue sphere, perhaps 60 metres in
diameter, which turns to green and finally red. Stunning.

*Aficionados* of fireworks should not miss the *festa* of Settefrati. The Sanctuary of the Madonna in Canneto, high in the
Apennines, is part of the *comune* of Settefrati. The statue of
the black Madonna spends her summers in the mountains

until she is carried back to Settefrati in procession on the evening of 22 August. Although the town of Settefrati is smaller than Gallinaro, the Madonna of Canneto has thousands of faithful adherents from all over the region, all of whom dig deep into their pockets for this *festa*. As the procession reaches the town the fireworks begin in earnest, and when she is finally home in her church the main event begins. Last year there were thirty-five minutes of pyrotechnic paradise, visible from most of the valley. This is a blessing, since Settefrati is almost inaccessible on that night because of the huge volume of cars and buses that start arriving throughout the afternoon.

The tradition of the market and the *festa* is part of what gives Italian life its unique flavour. Both of these public events are common and highly visible, their delights easily available to the visitor. A few days spent among Italians reveals a whole gamut of idiosyncrasies, uniquely Italian.

A visit to a bar provides examples aplenty. The function of a bar in Italy is not primarily to sell alcohol: there is food, coffee and tables at which to play cards. All over rural Italy men sit at bar tables playing *briscola, tressette* and *scopa*. This is a noisy activity, involving banging cards on the table, railing against ill-fortune, castigating your partner or opponent, and arguing with spectators' opinions about which card should have been led.

A visitor will quickly learn that a coffee, ordered and drunk standing at the counter, will cost very little; sitting at a table, it will cost more. How much more depends on where the bar is. In Sinella's bar I don't think there is any difference, but if the bar is in Piazza della Signoria in Florence, or Piazza San Marco in Venice, the difference is astronomical. Coffee is small, black and often already sugared on arrival – anything else must be specified. Standard sugar in Italy is as fine as caster sugar, while the salt is coarse. A peculiarity of bars is that they are full of children, running in and out buying

ice-cream and soft drinks. Bars appear to have no set closing time; as long as there is someone buying something, they will remain open. In the summer in Gallinaro this can mean as late as three a.m., and more often than not the children are still there, refusing to go to bed.

Paying in bars takes one of two forms. The old way, still the most common, is to order what you want, re-order again and again and only on leaving do you pay, never after each purchase. In the north of Italy and on motorways the pre-paid ticket is more common. First you go to the cash desk and queue, reel off your order, pay, then take the docket to the counter, queue, and reel off your order again. Shades of Moscow's Gum store.

Queueing in Italy is an art-form. It is not the ordered Anglo-Saxon file of first come, first served, rather a loose grouping with a common purpose. Most bus-stops appear to have no queues at first glance. Near the stop people idly browse in shop windows, or stand around in casual groups, generally giving the impression that the bus-stop is of no interest to them whatsoever. When a bus arrives, or rather if it does, there is a sprint for the door and a scrum. No quarter is given to the sick or elderly; whoever has the strongest elbows gets on. This is called *menefreghismo*, or, I'm all right,

Jack. Friends of mine who go to London delight in playing a simple game. On busy pavements they deliberately walk into a hapless Londoner and then giggle childishly when the Londoner says 'Sorry' instead of an Italian response such as, 'Why don't you look where you're going, arsehole?'

Queues in shops follow much the same pattern as at bus-stops. First served is he who gets to the counter first and catches the assistant's eye. To say, 'I think this lady was before me,' would be *fesso*. It is everyone for themselves and woe to the slow or polite.

At home, in private, the Italians are close. The need for personal space is not as important as it is in northern countries. Many households will consist of *mamma*, *babbo*, the *bambini*, *Nonno* and *nonna* and perhaps an odd *zia* as well. In this extended household of three or more generations the *bambini* are happy to remain until their late twenties. Despite appearances, *mamma* is the sole but benign ruler of this kingdom. The paterfamilias is accorded all kinds of small respects, such as being served first at meals, being given the choicest morsels, having his coffee sugared and stirred, his fruit peeled, his shoes polished and his general needs catered to by all the females in the household. He will also decide when the pasta is cooked to perfection. Do not be deceived; although accorded these symbols of power, the real *podestà* is *mamma*. She controls virtually all aspects of the household – its members and its economy. Women have real power in Italy, so they can afford to make small gestures to the male ego.

Most Italian women combine their role as mother with a job outside the home. To some extent this is facilitated by the structure of the standard working week – six hours a day, six days a week. Effectively this means that one parent can always be home from work in time to meet the children from school. State-run nursery schools take children from the age of three and give them lunch before busing them home. This makes it easier for both parents to have a job, secure in the knowledge that their children are not loose on the streets. Life in Italy is hard unless both partners in a marriage have a job. One income, unless enormous, leaves you near the poverty line.

Children spend a lot of time with their parents. Baby-sitting is a new concept, especially in our valley. Children accompany their parents everywhere – to restaurants, to parties, even to nightclubs, where they dance and stay up to all hours with the adults. Far from children being disapproved of in public places, they are welcomed with literally open arms. I remember eating in the Zi Teresa in Naples, a waterfront restaurant built over the sea, when my son was two or so. He was tired, bored and cross. Within moments the waiter had whisked him off to the kitchen, where he spent the evening, returning when we were leaving on the chef's shoulders, wearing the chef's hat. More than once strangers at other tables in restaurants have asked the children to join their tables, amusing the little dears until we had finished eating. I must confess that there were times when, after a long car journey accompanied by incessant squabbling on the back seat, this Italian indulgence of children came as a welcome relief. There is no doubt that Italy is an easier country to travel in with children than France or England. Far from making it harder to get a table in a restaurant, your chances are improved by small, tired faces demanding food.

People who worry that the European Community will lead us eventually to a pan-European culture with all national characteristics absorbed into a communal soup should take heart from Italy. Despite being an original signatory to the Treaty of Rome, it is no more German or French now than it ever was, nor, I am sure, will it ever be. The idiosyncrasies that make a country what it is have evolved over millennia; political and economic union will change little of that.

# 14

## *Religion*

I only once saw a Pope in the flesh. I was fifteen and the summer holidays were at an end. Our old family friends Memmo and Wanda Regoli were driving me to Rome airport from Sora. There was no *Autostrada del Sole* then; the road to Rome was the Casilina, through Frosinone, Anagni and Valmontone. It was in Valmontone, about half-way to Rome, that we came to a stop. Traffic was blocked and crowds swarmed. Like good Italians, instead of finding a way to proceed with the journey, we joined the crowds to find out what was afoot. Pope Paul VI was about to pass through in a motorcade. From my vantage-point at the side of the road I saw an open-topped car approaching slowly, with the Pope standing up between the front and rear seats. This is no easy place to stand and wave, even for a young and energetic man, so the Pope had help. Sitting directly behind him on the back seat was an aide, whose job was to keep his arms extended forwards and upwards while the Pope half-stood and half-sat on the outstretched hands. When we resumed our journey, Memmo taught me to say in Arpino dialect: '*Ho visto il Papa, e uno che teneva la mano sul culo.*'

This event made me realize that the Pope was a man, no more, no less. For all the trappings of majesty, he still needed a steadying hand on his bum. The inhabitants of Valmontone had enthusiastically turned out to see him, but were equally iconoclastic in their comments on his mode of travel. In many ways this is symptomatic of the Italian view of the papacy.

The largest single influence on life in the Comino Valley over the centuries has been the Roman Catholic Church. In central Italy this influence has been felt not only spiritually, but also in a very material sense, since the Church was for centuries its civil ruler. The Papal States varied in extent over the years, depending on the degree of acquisitiveness of the incumbent Pope, but most of the time the territory was a wide band across the middle of Italy acting as a buffer between the northern city-states and the southern Kingdom of the Two Sicilies – or the Kingdom of Naples, as it was known in its final years.

Italian history is full of battles, with Popes at the head of their armies leading crusades that were venal in everything but name. If you lived in the Papal States, the Pope was all-powerful in the realm of the spirit and of the body. His agents dispensed indulgences and absolutions for the soul, whilst other agents collected tithes, taxes and levied soldiers. There was no part of daily life that was not controlled or affected by the papacy; after so long a run – more than 500 years – echoes of the pontiffs' reigns are not hard to find.

To understand how the Roman Church has interacted with the Comino Valley, a little history is in order. The end of the Spanish viceregal rule, the decades of Austrian administration and the foundation of the Kingdom of Naples all had little effect upon the lives of the inhabitants of the Comino Valley. Life in the 1700s was much as it had always been in the preceding centuries, but a reasonably clear picture emerges of valley life as written records begin to be more abundant. In 1703 the population of Gallinaro stood at 492. This rather low figure is certainly the result of the Great Plague of 1656, which probably left the town with about 400 citizens. By the end of the century the population had reached 1,044 – about what it is today. This growth was partly organic, but partly due to the inclusion of the hamlet of Rosanisco in the 1795 census. Without that, Gallinaro's population had grown to approximately 750, so there was an increase of 50 per cent in a century. As a result of this population boom, the town began to spread southwards along the crest of the hill and pressure on the food supply began to be felt. The commonage in Rosanisco and Pietrafitta came into cultivation to help feed the swelling numbers. Emigration, noted as early as 1541, began in earnest. In the spring of 1764 half the inhabitants of San Donato, a neighbouring town, emigrated to Rome, Sonnino and Puglia. The Gallinarese who returned from the annual migration to the Pontine marshes brought back barely enough money to cover their taxes, and frequently malaria as well. A further tithe on the migrant workers was made when they changed their Roman money for ducats. In the early eighteenth century Bishop Gagliano of Sora issued decrees preventing officials from profiteering from exchange rates. 1764 was a year of famine in the valley, and Gallinaro parish records show that eighty people died that year, the majority with '*fame destitutus*' written against their name. As ever, famine affected only the poor.

It is worth recording the distribution of land ownership taken from the land registry of Charles III in 1744. The total acreage of Gallinaro amounted to 5,965, broken down as follows:

|                                | *acres* |
|--------------------------------|---------|
| Church                         | 2040    |
| Town council                   | 447     |
| Ducal estates                  | 77      |
| Local landowners               | 584     |
| Landowners from other towns    | 2817    |

The 584 acres belonging to the inhabitants of the town were divided among ninety-two families. The largest holding of 132 acres belonged to the Bevilacqua family. Ten families, including my ancestor Francesco di Tullio, had more than ten acres. The remaining 273 acres were divided among eighty-two families. Since the average family had eight members, this last figure means that some 650 people were trying to eke a living from less than 300 acres.

One advantage of longevity is the accrual of wealth, and the Roman Church is no exception. Over centuries dying penitents sought to ease their passage through the Gates of Saint Peter by bequeathing their land and assets to the Church, ensuring its position as the largest single landowner. Clearly those with fractions of an acre were unable to feed themselves or their families. To stay in the valley meant taking land in conacre from the Church. Land was rented out to the landless for approximately one third of a ducat per acre, which corresponded to one third of the value of an acre of corn. At first sight the rent was not extortionate, but it should be remembered that yields were far below today's, between three and five times the amount of grain planted. An old saying, 'O brigante, o emigrante' – either be a brigand or emigrate – first appeared at this time.

Daily life was governed by the exigencies of survival and what was outside these necessities was also under the control of the Church. Here are some of the decisions reached by the Sora Synod in 1714 as they affected the archparish of Gallinaro:

1   Teachers and lecturers in Arts and Letters had to profess their faith in the Church before they could work.

2   For any kind of public spectacle, theatre or recitation permission had to be got from the bishop.

3   Anyone selling books or paintings had first to obtain permission from the bishop.

4    The sale or preparation of food for oneself or for others was banned during the forty days of Lent.

5    Doctors were not allowed to visit a patient for a second time until the invalid had made a confession.

This sample of ecclesiastical law makes it clear how Church and state were inextricably linked both within the Papal States and outside them. Whatever activity could be perceived as relating to faith or morals was subject to Church control. One of Gallinaro's best-known archpriests, Bartolomeo Baldassari, much of whose writings are still extant, reported some young men to the ducal authorities for smiling at girls in his church, and another time denounced some men for swearing in public. There was almost no aspect of life that was not of concern to the Church.

The Church's main weapon of control was debt. In the parish records from 1826 to 1842 an average of 100 people a year appear in the debtors' ledger. The amounts are not large, up to a maximum of six ducats, but the same names and the same amounts appear annually under such headings as rent, taxes, food and religious expenses. It is clear that for many poor families their continued existence was dependent upon the clemency of the archpriest, since they were never in a position to completely clear their debt from one year to next.

The demographic breakdown of the area covered by the present-day province of Frosinone was, until recently, unchanged for centuries. By the middle of the nineteenth century the population was about 650,000. The poor and the unskilled made up nearly 30 per cent of this total, while the landed, the professionals and the merchants totalled about a tenth. The majority worked in agriculture and a little industry. Apart from industry, of which Gallinaro had none, the social divisions would have closely mirrored those of the region. The level of literacy was about 10 per cent, and was probably confined to the middle and upper classes, since the numbers closely correspond. Only a quarter of the literate were female.

For the poor and unskilled the only way out of a life that offered work during all daylight hours was emigration, brigandage or the seminary. The seminary represented a chance to learn, to better oneself. Thus was the Church able to maintain its position: by stick through debt and dependence, by carrot through offering a chance of betterment to the poor. What education was available outside the seminaries was rudimentary. It appears that it was also badly paid. My ancestor Dionisio di Tullio was the schoolmaster in Gallinaro in 1810. His remuneration was twelve ducats a year, equivalent to the yield from twelve acres, a bit less than £3,000 in today's money.

A picture emerges of a Church whose influence was almost limitless, until the unification of Italy reduced the Papal States to a few acres of Vatican City and began the division between Church and state. The Church's dominance as a major landowner began to decline as the state passed laws forcing the sale of Church land. By the turn of the century state education was more freely available. I have heard on several occasions a phrase attributed to Pius IX on signing the Concordat that left him with only the Vatican City: 'Beware of public education.' His instincts seem to have been correct, for the rise in literacy and the free dissemination of information has run parallel with a fall in the power of the Church. The fear of untrammelled education was balanced by the obligation on all pupils in state schools to attend religious instruction, which meant only Roman Catholicism. Children of Italy's religious minorities, although free to practise their own religion, were none the less constrained to learn about Catholicism. This was the law most fiercely defended by the Church, and only very recently has it been removed from the Civil Code. The 1990s began with a total division between Church and state – a situation that has never before existed in Italian history.

Of the great temporal power only the Vatican City remains. The picturesque Swiss Guards, so beloved of Vatican postcards, are the last visible vestige of papal might. The reason why the Pope's bodyguards are Swiss is in itself informative. Throughout the Middle Ages the most feared mercenaries were the Swiss. It is no accident that this small, mountainous country has not been invaded for so long. Apart from the fact that most rulers of any possible invading country had their money invested there, no one was too keen to take on the ferocious Swiss soldiers – especially in their own valleys and mountains. It was understood for centuries that if you wanted the best protection, you hired the Swiss. That the Popes did and still do speaks volumes for the temporal power invested in the papacy. Roman emperors unsure of the loyalty of their subjects often hired German mercenaries for personal protection. Perhaps the Popes hired the Swiss for the same reason.

Since the Comino Valley has historically been a remote pocket with little contact beyond its own boundaries, old traditions and cultural mores have survived longer than in other areas of Italy. My great-uncle, the archpriest Ferdinando Tullio, whose house we now live in, was probably the last to run his archparish in the old mould. He supervised all aspects of village life, from arranging marriages to recommending loyal parishioners for jobs. Just as in days gone by, he dispensed largesse to the poor of the parish, building up an account of favours due that perpetuated his position of authority. But even so remote a valley as mine could not withstand the onslaught of twentieth-century information technology. Even here new ideas eventually arrived, wreaking radical changes. Where once the archpriest of Gallinaro had several curates under his dominion, each with his own church, by 1992 Gallinaro did not even have a permanent priest. All churches, with the exception of the main church and the Sanctuary of Saint Gerardo, are now either abandoned, derelict or deconsecrated. The temporal power, once wielded with so large a stick, is gone. With its passing, the fear mingled with respect and awe of the Church's representatives has been replaced by apathy.

The change from total domination of daily life to a marginal position, similar to that of the Church of England, has been gradual but accelerating. My earliest memory of the church in Gallinaro is a congregation of women and children, with a few old men who sat at the back or smoked outside, just in earshot of the mass. Even this poorly attended gathering has diminished and the congregation is now made up of a few old women. Italians respect power. They are prepared to make arrangements to deal with the powerful in so far as they affect daily life. The obverse of this is that once an individual no longer has power, there is no further need to accommodate that person in one's own cosmos. The decline in the influence of the Church is a function of the growing awareness that closeness to the priest and his belief is no longer necessary to one's advancement in the world.

What this suggests is that the Church was never a focus of spiritual life, but rather through its secular structures a necessity for personal advancement. Had the emphasis been more upon the spiritual needs of the population and less upon the material, it is possible that today there would be many more adherents. The largest growing religious group in the Comino Valley is the Jehovah's Witnesses. It is inconceivable that this sect could have made any impact at all even as recently as thirty years ago. Whatever it is that they offer is obviously not something the Catholic Church provides. The majority of the population, in whose life religion plays only the most peripheral part, remain nominally Roman Catholic. This is no more than inertia; it now means so little to so many that making a change is more effort than they care to make.

What does need an explanation is why such large numbers attend religious *feste* and miracle sites such as the Baby Jesus of Gallinaro when the churches are so empty. A lot can be explained by the Italian predilection for theatre. Colourful processions and the prospect of witnessing a miracle are a lot more fun than sitting in a church. But it goes deeper than this. Carlo Levi in *Christ Stopped at Eboli* described how the inhabitants of that remote town, although nominally Catholic, were fundamentally pagan in their beliefs and superstitions. This paganism is by no means obvious in Gallinaro, but remnants can still be found.

The focus of Gallinaro's annual festival honouring San Gerardo is entirely Christian although the central image – the saint carried on his bier in procession – has pagan undertones. Pleas to the saint for intercession are accompanied by gifts of money and jewellery, which bedeck his statue on feast days. Quite what a statue is supposed to do with jewellery and cash is unclear to me, unless the saint in his heaven accepts offerings to his effigy as bribes to grant favours. Some of the money goes to the Church, of course. Each time San Gerardo goes walkabout, the episcopal office in Sora collects one million lire from the *festa* committee.

What San Gerardo has in common with many saints in Italy is that the local legends about him have little basis in history. Some years ago the Church tried to clean up a historical legacy of pagan gods masquerading as saints. The early Christian Church contended with strongly held beliefs in local deities. The cry 'Great is Diana of Ephesus' was heard with variations all over the Roman Empire. The founding fathers of the Church dealt with this by making the local deity a saint in the Christian cosmos. For example, Naples has San Gennaro, known as Janus in his previous incarnation as the Roman god of doorways and gates. The affection of Neapolitans for their patron saint, he of the liquefying blood, is strong. His statue, with its phial of congealed blood, is venerated, and, if he is slow to perform, he is encouraged with such entreaties as, 'Hey, yellow-face, get on with the miracles.' When the Vatican drew up its list of saints with thin claims to actual existence, San Gennaro was included. The idea was to demote from sainthood anyone who had probably never been alive. Saint Peter's Square was laid siege to by thousands of outraged Neapolitans, who were not slow to point out that Rome's Saint Lucy had equally slim credentials, but that she was omitted from the list and would remain a saint. The Vatican relented and, despite his pagan roots, San Gennaro is still the patron saint of Naples.

A further aspect of the Church's role over the centuries has been the behaviour of its agents, the priests. The enormous power that they once wielded was not always used for the benefit of the poor and the hungry. Priests through the ages amassed money and property. I still have documents belonging to Don Ferdinando, my great-uncle the archpriest, which relate to a loan made by him to a bus company in the 1930s. The amount was 30,000 lire, a huge sum, equivalent to about £70,000 in today's money. The question is, where did an archpriest of a small village get so large a sum? Although my family was never poor or landless, it never had access to amounts this big, so this was not a family inheritance. The answer appears to be that as archpriest he had the usufruct of the church lands, making him effectively the largest landowner in the village. This would be supplemented by his income from the Sunday plate, so accumulating such a large sum was not impossible. Sadly for Don Ferdinando's heirs, the money was never repaid.

On both my father's and my mother's side of the family, priests abounded. Don Francesco, known as Don Cicco, was a great-uncle to my mother. He lived in San Nazario in the Fusco family house. That he should be treated with kid gloves was never questioned. He was served meat daily, while the family ate the gravy on their pasta; he got the best wine, the choicest fruit. He was a big man, and proud of his physical strength, which far outstripped his intellectual gifts.

Even my father, aged ten, was moved to remark after serving mass for him that his Latin was abysmal. He is best known in family lore for the time the Bishop of Sora came to visit him with his Monsignor. Unable to follow the theological conversation over lunch, Don Cicco insisted on taking his two visitors out into the garden afterwards. Bending down, he picked up a huge tree-trunk and lifted it over his head. 'There,' he exclaimed proudly, 'I bet neither of you two smart-arses can do that.'

There have been priests in the valley who have built apartment blocks at seaside resorts and in the valley itself. It appears to have been normal for priests to amass wealth. If they still do, it is not reflected in the state of the churches themselves, which would probably have been in total disrepair by now had it not been for the earthquake rebuilding funds.

On a personal level priests have always been seen primarily as men and secondarily as celibate priests. The prevailing ethos was that celibacy meant a prohibition on marriage, rather than abstinence from sex. The spiritual, but above all the economic, power that these men held meant that their carnal desires could be easily accommodated in a poor, peasant society.

I have no doubt that there have been, and still are, good men who are priests. It is none the less true that today's legacy from the past is represented more by the deeds of the venal than of the benign. The speed at which the edifice is crumbling must be worrying to Rome. It is not just the dwindling congregations, but also the catastrophic decline in the numbers of applicants for the priesthood. The Curia's only hope must be for some kind of economic disaster, because as long as Italy basks in prosperity its people have less and less time for the Church. It is possible that economic adversity will drive Italians back to the churches – a survey in late 1993 suggests that this is the case.

Scandals involving the Vatican and the Banco Ambrosiano,

its connections with infamous Masonic lodge P2, and the imbroglio surrounding the death of Pope John Paul I made it clear to millions of Italians that, despite pretensions to piety, Vatican bureaucracy was no different from that found in town halls. Its connections with the corruption pervading the state were unbounded. This, too, has contributed to a change in perception that has led to the complete separation of Church and state. Constitutionally, the Church no longer has a say in governing the country. Despite opposition from the pulpit, both abortion and divorce are available to Italian citizens.

The physical evidence of the Church's decline is easy to find – empty, unkempt churches, tiny congregations, a lack of priests. What remains, and is harder to quantify, is the moral and ethical legacy of Catholicism. Social order and harmony exist around the globe even where Christianity is unheard of. Close family ties and love of children can be found to an identical degree in China. The staples of morality are universal and cannot be claimed to be exclusively Christian. There is no doubt that for many centuries the Church served as a unifying force between the disparate, independent city-states of Italy. Their common religion was a strong bond which ensured that, despite differences, a sense of Italianness was kept alive, transcending local loyalties. It could be argued that by keeping an overall sense of Italy living in the minds of Italians, the Church made unification a reality, thus creating a state that ultimately contributed to the Church's own decline.

Living in Ireland, I cannot help but be struck by the different attitude to the Vatican of Irish Catholics. Distance alters perception, and in the early years of Christianity it also made control difficult. The Celtic Church was largely autonomous and to some degree heterodox in its beliefs. Not until the Synod of Whitby in 664 did the Celtic Church come under Roman rule. Never being physically close to the Vatican, the Irish faithful were never privy to the worst excesses of medieval popes and cardinals. Only recently have scandals such as that of the Banco Ambrosiano found their way into print. The story of Bishop Eamonn Casey and Annie Murphy created shock waves in Ireland, whereas in Italy it would hardly have rated a mention. Proximity to the Church and the foibles of its officials has forged the Italian view – mostly apathy, with perhaps a little lingering respect. I would suspect that in Ireland, where a less accurate picture has been painted and promulgated for years, there will be more rage and less understanding when press self-censorship on the affairs of the Church is finally lifted.

It's tempting to draw parallels with the British monarchy, whose authority and patronage have also been pervasive. Both the Roman Church and the British monarchy have a long history of great power and extensive influence. Neither is adept at coming to terms with changed circumstance, both are obsessed with the grandeur of their respective inheritances. Blinded by a conviction that rigid conformity with tradition is the only path, both are staring oblivion in the eyes.

For the moment the Church commands respect because it has some power to wield; when its power goes, the respect will evaporate like the early morning mists. For the first time in many centuries it is possible to make a living in Italy without subscribing to the Catholic Church. Secularism, hand in hand with extreme consumerism, is the *Zeitgeist* of late-twentieth-century Italy.

# 15

# *Then and Now*

Even the most cursory look at southern Italy alerts the observer to some strange combinations. There is extraordinary beauty and extraordinary mess. Town planning seems to be embryonic and ineffectual. Half-finished buildings litter the countryside, finished apartment blocks wait years for a pavement and the removal of the builders' rubble. Large civic projects remain in a limbo of incompleteness for years and years. Roads that have been dug up stay like that for months. On the outskirts of towns there are haphazard areas of industrial estate, sprawling with no apparent overall plan.

There is a carelessness with rubbish; it can be found in streets, hedgerows and even in the most remote parts of the Abruzzi National Park. Not all of this is the fault of the citizens; new by-laws prevent the disposing of electrical white goods with domestic rubbish. Dumps won't take old fridges and washing-machines, but hedgerows will. Quite what else you are supposed to do other than dispose of these things furtively is anyone's guess.

The mountains of rubbish are a symptom of Italian consumer society. Italians have a lot of disposable income. The reasons for this are varied, but begin with the undoubted fact that the country is rich. My son learns in his Irish school that the south of Italy is chronically poor. The textbook that says this was not written in the 1950s but recently, so I am puzzled at how the author came to this conclusion. Perhaps he remembered it from the 1950s, when it was true. The fact is that this opinion, although common, is a fallacy. Italy's gross domestic product outstrips that of the UK, which is why it is a member of the G7. The south is poorer than the north, but it is only a question of degree.

The Italian Bureau of Statistics throws out some fascinating titbits. Italy is the largest importer in the world of Scotch whisky, diamonds, fur and luxury German cars such as BMW and Mercedes. This is not the purchasing pattern of a poor nation. These statistics become a reality to the observer of any street scene – most of these items are on prominent display.

What makes conflicting reports on the health of Italy's economy more understandable is the division between the poverty of the public purse and the wealth of individuals. Italy has been described as a poor country inhabited by rich people. The state has enormous trouble levying taxes on its recalcitrant citizens, relying almost totally on taxing expenditure. Thus petrol is, as far as I know, the most expensive in the world. Coupled with the fact that Italy has a car fleet of over 25 million – nearly one car for every two people – the revenue potential of this one tax becomes clear.

Over the last twenty years the economic boom that propelled Italy into the company of industrialized nations has had a dramatic effect on the Comino Valley. This area of Italy was traditionally known as the *terra di lavoro*, the land of work, because for centuries its poverty-stricken inhabitants were migrant workers; they were the navvies of Italy. Great civil-engineering projects such as the draining of the Pontine marshes took their work-force from here, as did many seasonal enterprises such as fruit and grape picking in the hinterland of Rome. Or people emigrated – to the big industrial cities of the north, to other countries. The figures are mind-boggling. Over the last 100 years more than 3 million have emigrated from Lazio alone. These are the people whose ice-cream parlours and restaurants fill towns and cities all over Europe, as well as their more varied enterprises in the United States.

Some have made their mark on history. Domenico Pignatelli and Rosa Arpino are immortalized in stone; they were Rodin's models for 'The Kiss'. Some years ago another Rosa, an old friend, invited my wife and me back to her house for coffee. As she went into the kitchen we idly scanned the walls. In a corner, behind a door, was a small oil painting of a vase of flowers. Something about it made us look closer. When Rosa came back with coffee, we asked about it.

'Oh, that was done by a French artist, Rodin. My great-grandfather was one of his models. We've got five of them, I think.'

It transpired that these had been in part-payment for modelling, but unfortunately three of them were badly damaged. They had been buried during the war to protect them from the Germans, who were not averse to a little pillaging.

The effect on the Comino Valley of emigration was initially impoverishing. The young and the entrepreneurial left to begin new lives, new fortunes, elsewhere. As the years went by these emigrants enriched the valley, not only economically, but also by bringing back new ideas and customs. The twenty or so villagers who went to Paris at the turn of the century to model for Utrillo, Monet, Manet and Rodin brought home to Gallinaro a refreshing blast of French liberalism. This has left Gallinaro to this day the most secular of all the valley towns. Others have been great benefactors, subsidizing *feste*, rebuilding chapels, or supporting activities for the young, like football teams. The valley's inhabitants have learned more of other countries through the emigrants, and increasingly visit these countries themselves, which has led to a growing awareness that life in the valley has much to recommend it. It is at least as attractive as a sprawling *banlieue* of Paris. The lurking inferiority complex that emigration caused is being replaced by pride.

Increasing leisure has changed life in the valley. Now every village has a football pitch, tennis courts and running tracks, all built within the last fifteen years. Where once the only sport was *boccia*, the Italian *boule*, now the list is comprehensive. There are thirty-six sports clubs in the valley, covering activities from hang-gliding to kung fu. Not many years ago children were taken out of school to help with the harvest; now they fill their leisure time go-karting, skiing, swimming and eventing.

When I was first old enough to be aware of my surroundings, in the early 1960s, the valley was still much as it had always been. There were few cars; people travelled only when necessary, either to market or to hospital, by bus or taxi. The blue single-deckers that served the area were reasonably frequent, and always packed with people, rabbits in wicker baskets, chickens and ducks. Once I saw an old woman with a lamb. Taxis were private cars hired out with the driver. The more affluent would take a taxi if there were at least four going to the same destination. It was a peasant society with peasant values, rather like the rural Balkans of today. It was a common sight to see women walking the road, ramrod straight, carrying loads of wood or produce on their heads, often accompanied by their husband astride a donkey, smoking a pipe. Small children had the job of driving the sheep and goats along the road, at dawn and dusk, to and from the pastures. Watching this made me understand the saying about separating the sheep from the goats. In England it seems to make little sense: sheep look nothing like goats, any idiot can tell the difference, whereas the sheep in the Comino Valley are long-legged and more hairy than woolly – like goats. You have to look very hard to tell the difference.

Those early years were when I first came across the 10-watt electric light bulb. They were common in the houses that had electricity and in public places such as bars, emitting about as much light as a guttering candle. Through the clear glass the element glowed a dull red, its sole virtue being its minimal consumption. Nothing was wasted, care was taken with everything. Bottles of all shapes and sizes were kept and washed; thinnings from the vines or fruit bushes were bundled into faggots for kindling; every scrap of land was coaxed into growing something. These were the outward manifestations of a state of mind: everything had to be nurtured, encouraged to yield something that might make life a little more comfortable.

In this world there was no room for the non-productive. To keep a dog as a pet was madness; a dog will eat as much as three hens and gives no eggs. There were no flower gardens, just the occasional geranium in a pot. Any scrap of land was required to produce vegetables. Trees were planted for nuts or fruit – there are still almost no evergreens in the valley. Nothing was thrown away, food scraps were composted or fed to the hens or pigs.

Many of the traditional dishes have simply evolved from the methods of preserving the year's crop when there was no electricity for refrigeration. Preserving tomatoes by boiling or making salted sausages for air curing was not a solitary occupation; because of the quantities involved, the neighbours had to help, so each family helped the others in these tasks. Life was simple and co-operative most of the time. There were no discos or hotels, there was only work, a day at the market or a game of cards in the bar.

I report this because the prosperity that cloaks the valley today has changed people's perceptions only superficially. People over the age of forty are still adjusting to the new world of consumerism and wealth. Several things follow from the novelty of prosperity. On the one hand people now delight in spending ostentatiously; on the other there is an abhorrence of anything that recalls the poverty of old. Not so long ago only people with money to spend bought white bread. Because it was made from wheat which is not grown in the valley, it had to be bought at a bakery rather than be made at home. The poor had red bread, made with flour from the maize that they grew themselves. Red bread is delicious, but no one eats it now; it can only be found in bakeries in Rome, where it carries no stigma of poverty.

Every house had a bread oven, built into a corner next to the hearth, using the same chimney. It was traditionally at waist level; the space underneath held the wood. Like a pizza oven, the inside was domed and you either lit a fire in the oven to bring it up to temperature, or you took embers from the fire and shovelled them in. Monday was the day for baking. Seven large 2-kilo loaves were made, and usually some pizza as a treat. These loaves were kept in wooden chests with high legs designed to discourage rodents, wrapped in linen. By Sunday you needed good teeth for these *pagnotte*, hard enough to eat when fresh, but dense and tough after a few days. Before bottled gas arrived in any quantity, country kitchens had stoves which were heated by charcoal, or, if not, the cooking was done on the open hearth. Beans were cooked in a terracotta jug, placed at the side of the hearth and left overnight.

Very little food was bought. All fruit and vegetables came from the *orto*, the garden, and every household kept rabbits and hens. Meat was not an everyday item, although a careful cook was able to use tiny off-cuts of pork to flavour the *sugo*, the tomato sauce for the pasta. With care a pig could be made to last a year – even the skin on the cured hams, hard as leather, was used to flavour the sauce. In times of real hardship it was not unknown for the skin to be used over and over again, even lent to neighbours as a kind of soup stone. In wine, too, people were self-sufficient. A tenth of a hectare planted with a local high-yielding grape will produce about 1,000 litres in a good year, sufficient for a family's yearly supply.

With 50 litres of olive oil, maize for polenta and red bread, beans and the occasional supplement of poultry, the staples for what was essentially a healthy diet were all there. Very little refined sugar was eaten, only fruit and honey, so even the very old kept their teeth. This diet, combined with physical work in the fields, produced a hardy race, strong, wiry and long-lived. The older women in the valley walk just as osteopaths tell us to do today: straight-backed from years of balancing loads on their heads.

Only now are the old, traditional ways of doing things beginning to be appreciated. As soon as the first glimmerings of prosperity arrived, kitchens were torn apart, shiny Formica cupboards replaced the old *credenze*, hearths and brick ovens were replaced with bottle-gas cookers and heaters. In the mad scramble for modernity, in the rush to become part of the twentieth century, ugly, tacky, mass-produced tat took the place of artisan-made things. Hundreds of traditional chairs, ladder-backed with raffia seats, were discarded to make way for tubular steel; wardrobes were exiled to hen-coops as built-in laminated chipboard cupboards took their place. Today people are beginning to question their haste. Antique and curio shops are making an appearance, although they are still treated with some circumspection. I overheard one well-dressed matron say, 'I know it's very old, but it isn't *used*, is it?'

Perhaps the biggest contribution to the changes in the social life of the village has been made by Benito Colarossi. He returned to the valley from Scotland in the 1970s and built the Hotel Tramps on the *superstrada* that links San Donato and Atina. Its arrival coincided with the wave of prosperity sweeping the valley. Tourism is non-existent in the Comino Valley, so the bulk of Colarossi's business was, and still is, receptions.

Italians have always spent money on weddings. Even the poorest saved for years to ensure their daughters had not only a 'bottom drawer' – six or sometimes twelve of every sort of household linen – but a wedding to remember as well. Where once in Gallinaro these celebrations took place at home, now they are held in the hotel. Numbers have increased exponentially; it is not unusual to have 500 or more guests eating ten courses at the wedding feast. What are new are the baptismal feasts, the confirmation feasts, celebrations for passing the baccalaureate or getting a degree. Last year there was a dinner for the first anniversary of a baptism.

Not only do these celebrations place a burden on the hosts, they also cost the guests money. It is now general practice at weddings in the valley to give as much money as the meal costs per head. Thus if husband and wife go to a reception, that is 100,000 lire each, plus a present. Not surprisingly, as the economic situation gets more austere, people are finding excuses for not attending, or the husband or wife goes alone, halving the cost. Refusals are difficult, because offence is taken. I have heard of people refusing to do further business with someone who had declined an invitation. It is therefore as much an obligation as an honour to be invited, hence the huge guest lists.

Gifts on occasions such as these are not small. A twelve-year-old in Gallinaro got three mountain bikes at his confirmation dinner, amongst other presents. The total outlay for all concerned is astronomical. Had this child been fourteen, the gifts would undoubtedly have included a motor bike. All children from the age of fourteen are permitted to have a *motorino*, and they all do. These are 50 cc mopeds; they must have no more than three gears and a top speed of less than 40 kilometres an hour. The best can cost as much as a small car, up to £5,000. The children are as fashion-conscious as their parents and wouldn't be seen dead on a *motorino* that was not the current model. Many companies cater to this market: Aprilia, for example, make stunning 50 cc bikes, one a fully fared racing bike, another a scrambler and, my favourite, the Red Rose, a Harley-Davidson look-alike with chrome all over it. Like all Italian design, these bikes really look the business, even if they don't go over 25 miles an hour.

Compared with twenty years ago when hardly anyone had a car in the valley, this is change indeed. It is not unusual for young adults to be given a car on their eighteenth birthday; in the valley the preferred choice is a four-wheel drive, a *fuoristrada*. By the time marriage comes around they will also be given a house to live in. In Italy home-ownership is universal, there is one house for every two inhabitants, so it is evident that many of these are second homes, either in a mountain resort or by the sea. Because they are almost all owned outright, the effects of high interest rates which cripple home owners in other countries have little effect in Italy. The ability to finance this is largely a result of the Italian family's *modus vivendi*. Because families stay together in one house, savings accrue until it becomes possible to build or buy another house with little or no mortgage. The same household economies, the lack of waste, the careful husbandry, allow Italians a large disposable income, which, like everything else, is carefully husbanded in savings.

This fact explains why Italy's enormous state debt has not had the same crippling effect as it has had in other countries. Ninety-seven per cent of the state's debt is internal. The borrowing has been against the savings of the citizens, not in Deutschmarks, and so devaluing the lira has not been catastrophic.

The vast increase in spending-power has not been confined to individuals. The state has appropriated its share and some of it has been spent on infrastructure. Despite the continuing revelations of corruption and graft in all levels of the state's administration, clearly not all the money went into lining the pockets of the officials. Once the only task that a town hall could be seen to be doing was providing dim street lights. But then the resources were minuscule. Today Italy's *comuni* are well funded, so well that graft and waste are their common currency. It is quite possible that the current trend towards financial rectitude and austerity will put an end to many of the more outrageous profligacies of the administrations.

As an example, despite the fact that there is hardly a soul without motorized transport, in 1991 a new bus service was introduced in the valley, paid for by the Lazio region. Four bus companies, based in the four largest towns of the valley, run shuttle services all over the area. An empty one passes through Gallinaro four times a day and I have never seen a passenger on board. These mini-buses roam the byways of the valley, serving, as far as I can see, no one at all. Since no one thought it necessary to co-ordinate the timetables of the various routes, it is virtually impossible to make connections, making a trip from one town to another a lengthy process. Still, this is the kind of government waste where at least the operators benefit, if no one else.

Town halls are now the providers of school buses, rubbish collection, urban sanitation, sewers and cultural events. This last is a new departure for the valley. In a strictly peasant society there was little room for culture in any form. The few educated people were necessarily better off than anyone else, so they could afford trips to Rome or Naples for the opera or theatre. For the majority, barely literate, these were luxuries they could neither afford nor understand. The contempt in which the *contadini*, the peasants, were held was remarkable. Because they could not read or write and had implicit trust in their social superiors, they were ripped-off continually. The concept of *noblesse oblige* had no currency in the valley. Many of those who had education and positions of privilege used both unscrupulously to further their own ends. Even today the elderly poor are often treated with scorn by minor officials such as bank clerks when they have failed to fill in some form correctly. The enormous popularity of the Communist party, until recently, is largely a result of this kind of treatment.

All this historical baggage makes sense of much of what happens today. The flashy clothes, the jewellery, the new cars, all affirm publicly how far the owner has come from the land. Thinking about it now, I realize how odd I must have sounded when I regaled everyone with tales of my newly discovered bucolic bliss in the Wicklow hills. Chopping wood and growing food was exactly what everyone was trying to leave behind. My thatched roof must have sounded like a wilful return to the Stone Age. When you bear this in mind, the concreting of the old houses in the village takes on a different hue. What looks picturesque to a visitor is uncomfortable, draughty and cold to the inhabitant. How much better to have a roof that needs no maintenance, aluminium windows that keep out draughts, walls that don't crumble. How good not to live in an old house.

Some years ago an old farmer came to visit me. He stood in the hall looking around and his eyes fell on a pair of *cioce* – the traditional footwear – that I had hanging on a wall. 'They may look picturesque to you,' he said, 'but if you'd had to wear them, they wouldn't be on display.'

Now that the basics such as housing and education are no longer priorities, there is a growing interest in culture in all its forms. The *comuni* of the valley have been quick to satisfy this desire. Most of them have set up a *pro loco*, an official centre designed to co-ordinate and organize cultural activities. As a result of this impetus, there are now museums that catalogue the valley's history over the millennia; there are exhibitions of painting and sculpture, drama groups and an increasingly prestigious literary prize, the Premio Valle di Comino, administered from Alvito. There is even a growing awareness of ecology – Alvito runs the annual tree *festa*, as well as organized mountain walks; Picinisco has its mountain festival; San Donato its Nature Awareness week. Until recently a cultural wasteland, the valley is now farther ahead than any comparable area that I know elsewhere in Europe. In the gazetteer published by the valley's tourist office (an oxymoron if ever there was one) there are over 200 hundred exhibitions and competitions listed throughout the year. In the short span of twenty years not only has the financial and social life of the valley undergone profound change, so too has its cultural life.

Before this explosion of awareness Arpino was the only cultural oasis in an agricultural desert. It lies just beyond the Comino Valley, but its ties to the valley are many and ancient. Arpino was the birthplace of Marius – the general and reformer of the Roman army – and of Agrippa, Octavian's general at Actium and the builder of the Pantheon, and of Cicero. For centuries it was the administrative capital that governed my valley, and for years a major industrial centre that gave employment to a wide hinterland. It has always been prominent historically for my own family. My parents' first encounter was in Arpino. Because their schoolfriends were here, some of my earliest memories are of visiting this town.

Today Arpino is the artistic and cultural capital of southern Frosinone. The new senator for this contituency is Massimo Struffi, who has injected a huge amount of energy in re-establishing his town as a centre for the arts. The Mastroianni Foundation, now located in the Castello di Ladislao, is here largely as a result of Struffi's efforts. Arpino has been a rich town for 2,000 years, and for this reason it has a very different feel from any of the others near the valley. Its architecture is more grand, more beautifully embellished. Its piazza is covered in travertine and is now adorned with the sculptures of Umberto Mastroianni, Marcello's uncle. The houses have the gloss of centuries of wealth, and the narrow, hilly streets have an air of quiet good taste. At first glance it has the look of a Tuscan town, a small jewel set in the hills of Ciociaria.

My earliest memories of simplicity and poverty seem like recollections from another era, another world. The farmhouse at San Nazario is no longer a working farm, the river that bounds it now has no water in the height of summer. In Gallinaro the public wash-rooms where the women gathered to wash their clothes and chat are gone; no one washes their clothes in the Rio Molle by bashing them between stones as countless generations had before. Tarmacadamed roads reach where once only mules walked, hillocks sprout new buildings on every slope. Ponte Melfa, a tiny hamlet twenty years ago, is a thriving town. Everywhere you look there is evidence of human activity. Ox-carts and mules used as beasts of burden are almost entirely gone – small tractors have replaced them all. I suppose what I have witnessed has been the demise of the peasantry. The new structures that have replaced the old are far from perfect, but for the common man they represent a leap forward of centuries. No doubt their rough edges will be less apparent as time goes by, as people begin to forget how it was and simply live with how it is. Photographs of Gallinaro that I took ten years ago could have been taken 200 years ago, so much has changed since and so little before. In the Comino Valley the world of the *contadino* has all but vanished, leaving only scattered vestiges of centuries of tradition.

# 16

## Damming the Molarino

Anyone who has seen the film *Jean de Florette* will know what I mean when I say that water is important. Rainfall is sparse in the Comino Valley; what water we have during the long, dry summer is provided by the snow melting in the high Apennines. One main river flows almost the length of the valley, rising in the mountains above Settefrati. This is the Melfa, which joins the Liri near Roccasecca. A tributary, the Molarino, rises above San Biagio at the eastern end of the valley and joins the Melfa below Atina at Ponte Melfa, the Melfa turquoise green and the Molarino steely grey. There are a few small streams, such as Gallinaro's Rio Molle, but otherwise this represents the water available to the valley's inhabitants. If the mountains surrounding the valley are free of snow in April, water will be scarce in the summer, since rain cannot be relied on to keep the rivers flowing.

Obviously water usage is controlled − it is metered and expensive, and mains water is not available all day. Sometimes in the summer the mains can be on for as little as three hours in the early morning. To make life bearable, most houses, including my own, have a large water tank which fills while the mains is flowing. In my case the system is then powered by what the Italians call an *autoclave*, a pump which pressurizes all the pipes to 2 atmospheres. On paper the system is great, in practice it needs endless adjustment and care.

Once water was supplied by the *comune*. A few years before Thatcherism became popular in Britain, the *comune* sold its distribution system to a semi-private concern, the Aurunci. This company now supplies the water to the village and reaps handsome rewards for its efforts. Recently it has started charging the *comune* for the water it supplies to the drinking fountains, so they are slowly being removed – we are down to three. Fountains have been a feature of public places in Italy for more than 2,000 years; they are cool oases in the summer where a passing thirst can be slaked. Removing them removes not only a convenience, but a long, unbroken tradition.

Gallinaro's water comes from Canneto, the source of the Melfa, in the mountains behind Settefrati. From here the Aurunci pipe it to the towns that no longer provide their own supply. The pipe to Gallinaro runs up to the town under the road from San Donato. For years the road was a mess because of badly jointed piping that leaked continually. The leaks destroyed the sub-structure of the road, and the many attempts to patch up the faults left the road even worse. Like many Italian running sores, this one ran and ran. It took seven years before the water company decided to do the job properly and repair the road. Oddly, no one in the village ever seemed as angry about it as me; people shrugged, and tried to avoid the pot-holes.

On arrival at the village the water goes into a large and very ugly water tower. The story of this tower is fairly typical of civic projects, not just in my village, but all over southern Italy. It was decided, logically, that the tower should be situated at the highest point in the village. Since the old church occupied that site, the next best, a small hillock behind the cemetery, was chosen. The only encumbrance to this plan was the eleventh-century church of San Leonardo, which was in the way. Once it was the shepherds' church – it was outside the town walls, thus keeping the smelly shepherds out of the town centre. It hadn't been used for years, and anyway it was old, so the obvious course of action was taken: it was bulldozed, the top of the hill was levelled by removing all the topsoil, and the water tower was built, a giant *phallus impudicus* visible from just about anywhere. The flat area around the tower was designated a public park, the only problem being that nothing grows since all the topsoil has gone, and there is no easy path to get there. Still, rather like those Eastern European countries that issued postage stamps commemorating their satanic mills, you can buy colour postcards of the water tower in the mini-market.

The Apennines that surround the valley are made of limestone. A careful look at the white rock reveals the fossils of all the tiny sea creatures compacted to create these mountains. Since the Apennines are the source of the rivers, the water is high in lime. When the summer comes and the rivers run very low or dry up completely, all that is left is a brilliant white slash cutting through the valley, the stones of the river bed dazzling in the bright sun. From late June onwards, both the Melfa and the Molarino have no flow at all much beyond Ponte Melfa. More and more is being extracted for irrigation, leaving no more than the odd pool of gasping trout. Even that small flow is threatened by a new scheme to provide irrigation; it will leave both these water courses bleached, barren wildernesses.

Since the 1930s there has been a plan to create an artificial lake in the valley directly below my house. The soundings have all been made, the project has been appraised and considered for sixty years. It has also been argued about interminably in Sinella's bar. The source of contention is the purpose of the lake. It is not planned as an amenity for the valley, but is to provide water for irrigating the plains of Roccasecca, well beyond the valley to the south-west. What makes the villagers so angry is that the lake would be closed to the public, so there would be no fishing, no boating and no swimming. What there would be is mosquitoes. Since the lake would be slowly emptied during the hot months, the muddy banks would be exposed, providing an ideal breeding ground for the insects. However, I would stake my life on the fact that all the argument has no purpose, for the lake will never be built. If the money couldn't be found to do it when times were good, there is no chance now.

In the heat of summer my mind turns on only one thing. I need water to plunge into. Ever since I was a small boy the only solution to this urge was to get up extremely early in the morning and go to the sea. The early rise was vital to miss the heat while driving and to find a parking place. The nearest coast to us is the Tyrrhenian – Formia, Gaeta and Terracina being within reach. In the 1970s we got a *superstrada* from Cassino to Formia, which made life easier, and more recently we have a *superstrada* from the valley to Cassino, making the trip easier still. The only problem is the crowds. Italians seem to find twenty lines of beach umbrellas an acceptable environment, whereas for me it is a vision of hell. Over the years I have explored every little cove, nook and cranny from Terracina to Scauri, and every one of them is known to every Roman and Neapolitan, and they're packed.

I had solved the problem by simply not going to the beach, but as my children got older they wanted to swim. One summer we tried lakes. There is a beautiful lake at Posta Fibreno, at the western end of the valley. You can hire pedaloes, there are bars, it's amazingly pretty and the water is marginally above freezing. No matter how hot you get, three inches over the ankles is all the average man can take of this. It's frustrating, the water is so clear, it looks so right – and yet it's just too cold for swimming.

I bought a military map, which showed minor roads and

tracks that give access to ponds and lakes. On the map was an obvious candidate, Lago di Barrea. This is up in the Abruzzi National Park, not too far as the crow flies, but a long winding trip by road of just over an hour – about the same as going to the beach. We packed a picnic and left for the mountains, driving through San Donato, through the pass at Forca d'Acero and into the National Park. The highest point is just under 1,200 metres above sea-level. The road passes through the beech forests that cover the mountains where we go cross-country skiing. From the pass the road drops down towards the Sangro Valley, a vista that suddenly opens before you after leaving behind the heavily forested roadsides. The first sight to greet you in the National Park other than trees is the town of Opi. As the road makes a sharp left-hand turn you see it, exactly the shape of a coffin, stretched along the crest of a hill, laid out before you. These mountains and this valley have always been unspoilt wilderness and are still today the preserve of bears and wolves.

When my father was a young man there were partridge and ptarmigan in these mountains and he used to come here by horse to camp out and shoot. At that time this whole area was inaccessible by car; on horseback or on foot was the only way to get here. Every time I see Opi from here I remember my father's story of a hunting trip with his dog, Volpe. Vipers are a hazard in these mountains; a walk off the beaten path requires high leather boots for protection and a syringe of snake serum in the pocket. My father accidentally disturbed a viper and Volpe rushed in to defend him, taking the bite. With Volpe on his shoulders my father walked to Opi to find an old hunter that he knew who had the antidote. By the time he arrived four hours later, Volpe was in rigor and the outlook was bleak. Father left Volpe with the old man and went home, knowing that the dog was close to death. For a week the old man nursed the dog, for the first three days turning the dog from one side to the other every four hours, day and night. When my father returned, more in hope than expectation, it was early in the morning, barely daybreak. The houses were shuttered, nothing stirred. As he began the steep climb up the main street through the village a wild barking began from the other end, shortly followed by the descent of a galloping Volpe, wagging and yelping a greeting.

At the bottom of the hill is the Sangro river, where we turn right for the town of Villetta Barrea. Beyond lies the lake. The whole look and feel of this valley is very different from mine. It is entirely pastoral, the local economy still as it ever was: milk and cheeses, and of course timber. The air is far cooler here than it would be at the beach, and the lake looked tempting as we arrived. As it turned out, the lake has no obvious shoreline, at least not in summer. Before you can reach water deep enough to swim in, there is a long walk, ankle deep, through marshy reed beds, mud oozing between your toes. The heat made us all keen to swim, but this was not a perfect arrangement. As far as I can remember we only went there twice.

The lack of water was getting to us. We all agreed that staying in Gallinaro would be amazing if only there was somewhere to swim. My friends couldn't understand my problem. 'There are two big swimming pools in Gallinaro, in Tramps and in the Oasis. Go to one of them.' These pools exist all right, but if you ever thought the Italian Riviera was crowded, you haven't seen these pools. The noise level almost approaches that of physical pain and you can smell the chlorine from the car park. I wouldn't swim here by invitation, let alone pay heavily for the privilege. My wife succumbed to the children's entreaties on a few occasions and took them, but, like me, chlorine and noise is not her idea of heaven.

It seemed insurmountable. Building our own pool behind the house would be an amazing solution, but financially it was a non-starter. Anyway, it would have to be a very small pool in order to fit. I thought I had it licked when I found a large, fold-away plastic pool in a shop in Atina. We set it up in the garden, filled it with nearly one thousand litres of expensive water and jumped in. It was great water for splashing in, too small for anything more than two strokes, but at least it was on our doorstep for whenever we felt like it. Unfortunately after two days the water was green and smelly and the pool developed a leak. Another idea bit the dust.

That night, lying in bed, it came to me. Many years ago a cousin from Casalattico had taken me to the upper reaches of the Molarino where some huge concrete barriers had been built to control the raging torrents of winter which continually threaten to undermine the bridges that span it. It was a hazy memory, but I was sure we could find the place.

The next day we drove along the road to San Biagio, turning down any road or track that looked as though it might go towards the river. Occasionally we got near the water, but there was just a shallow trickle, not what we were looking for. And then we found it. Not exactly as I remembered, because the large concrete barriers lay smashed, broken like kindling. Whatever flood had done this must have been pretty ferocious. Behind one broken barrier we found a pool deep enough to get into. What flow there was fell into it from three feet above, creating a mini jacuzzi. Things were looking up. The children shouted: further upstream they had found a much larger pool, deeper and wider. Someone had used river stones to make a shallow dam, deepening the pool a little. The water was refreshingly cool in the midday heat, very clean and very clear. We swam until half-past one, alone in the Molarino, with no sight or sound of anyone else. Apart from the pool, the river bed was dry for nearly all of its width, a brilliant white-stoned highway slicing through the forest which lined its banks. Looking upstream, the purple shape of Monte Cavallo was framed perfectly by the trees on either side. Heaven.

By two o'clock the people who had built the stone dam arrived. We knew that was who they were because they had a proprietorial look about them that told us to shift. We moved to the smaller pool and made do. Over the next few days we found that the locals did not arrive until two: we had the use of the big pool until then. It wasn't that they were ungracious, only that this was obviously where they had come for the past fifty summers, and who were we to invade? The daily temperatures were in the mid-thirties, so we came here with our picnic lunch day after day.

I am by nature gregarious, and, like a child, not very good at keeping discoveries secret – especially exciting ones like this. My wife recognizes this failing and begged me to tell no one in Gallinaro of our find.

'Remember the skiing, and how we started a craze? They'll all be down here if they find out and we won't have it to ourselves any more.'

It was hard, but I managed not to tell anyone. Occasionally we were asked where we spent the day. 'Down at the Melfa,' I would lie. One afternoon, lying sunbathing on the flat surface of a broken barrier, I noticed that where the water flowed out of our small pool, it passed through a gap downstream with high sides made of piles of river stones and broken concrete barriers. I decided to build a dam there and make ourselves a really good pool.

Living in the Irish countryside has taught me over the years some useful skills – dry stone wall-building for one. My dam would be about 6 metres wide and as high as possible, constructed out of the white stones of the riverbed. My son and I began the construction by laying two lines of the biggest stones we could move across the gap about a metre apart. The space between the lines we filled with small stuff and gravel. It worked – the level rose by 5 centimetres. All this plan needed for success now was hard work. Two days into this hydraulic engineering project an Irish friend, Morrough Kavanagh, arrived for a visit on his way back to Dublin from Leipzig. With this extra pair of hands the dam rose majestically to just under a metre. Now we had a swimming pool, the best on the river. By this stage we had come to know the local bathers, who were encouraging and appreciative of our efforts, not least because it took the pressure off their pool.

Unfortunately our dam became local news. People came to see it during construction and after we had finished. Within a week of completion it had become public property. We had to arrive early to lay out towels and impedimenta to stake our claim. After about two weeks of increasing popularity, we arrived one day to find about thirty teenagers with loud ghetto-blasters and six-packs partying in our pool. Reluctantly we forced ourselves upon our friends upstream.

After a while we watched the intruders using the top of the dam as a diving board. The inevitable happened – it collapsed. Our Italian companions were outraged. *'Delinquenti!'* they yelled. *'Maleducati!'* A delegation was despatched in the shape of a five-year-old to find out what they thought they were doing. 'These people spent a month building that, and you've destroyed it in a day.' They seemed to be genuinely more concerned and angry than I was.

The child came back and announced, 'They say they're not delinquents. They broke it, and they're going to repair it.' I'll give them their due, they did try, but the rush of water through the break combined with their total lack of expertise with dam-building made it a hopeless task. I certainly felt no compunction to start again.

We went back a few more times, but the level of water

was down and, well, it just wasn't the same. Occasionally, though, good things come from misfortune and this turned out to be one of those occasions. We decided to look for a new spot higher up the river. The water gets significantly cooler the closer to the source you go, but there is also more of it since there is no irrigation upstream. In the summer the Molarino looks as tame as a pussy cat, a quiet trickle gently flowing over its exposed stony bed. During the winter it is a wild torrent of white-water erosion. As a defence against this, gabions line the banks where the pressure is greatest and barriers like the ones downstream have been built, but taller and wider. There is a section of river where three of these form waterfalls 6 metres or so high, one after the other. We found El Dorado when we reached the upper one after a long walk from the road.

This is precisely the area described by D. H. Lawrence in *The Lost Girl*, in the valley below the house that he had rented. It is a part of the Comino Valley that is still wild and overgrown. The area around the highest of these falls is densely forested and even in the hottest summers there is abundant greenery surrounding the waterfall. It looks like a huge sheet, cascading steely grey and foamy into a deep pool that is conveniently lined on one side by a sandy beach. By the time we had made this discovery, I had broken my vow of silence and our friends from Gallinaro had started to come with us. Despite the fact that Italians are not very good at immersing themselves in water whose temperature is below blood-heat, the place is so beautiful that even they succumbed to its charms. Once we had found this place, all thoughts of sea or swimming pools evaporated, all of us deciding that this was the *ne plus ultra* of bathing. It became even more attractive when, after some exploration, we found an old track that allowed us to get the car right up to the river.

A new place to eat is an exciting discovery in Italy. We

decided that here was where we should spend *ferragosto*, the
August bank holiday that is traditionally spent picnicking in
the great outdoors. Every year people sit around endlessly
discussing their plans for the bank holiday, ideas are floated,
and gradually loose groups form, vaguely committed to a

particular idea. Vaguely is the operative word here; I have never yet been on one of these expeditions where the group assembled on the day bore any relation to the one that had arranged to be there.

Small villages like ours are surprisingly democratic when it comes to parties or outings. It is assumed that anyone who hears of a planned event and who likes the sound of it is welcome to come along. There is no concept of invitation: if it is discussed in public, then it is public. This is entirely admirable and in the past I have behaved like this myself. This time, however, we were all concerned to limit the numbers out of pure selfishness and out of a desire to keep our discovery as much as possible a secret. Amazingly, when the day came, we were less than twenty.

Being able to bring the cars meant that a full-scale picnic was possible. Tables, chairs, loungers, sun-beds, cookers, pots and pans were unpacked at the river. Tommaso discovered a plant with huge leaves perfectly shaped for a sun hat, effective but extraordinarily foolish to behold. Graziano carefully arranged the deckchairs in the shallows, so it was possible to take the sun with feet in the cool water. Cessidio arranged an expedition to gather firewood, since we had lamb to cook. Diodato found a spot in the river where he put all the wine, beer and fruit to keep it cool. Friends arrived gradually, each unloading more food and drink. By midday the adventurous amongst us had taken the first plunge and it was time to eat.

At the open fire Cessidio presided over the lamb, carefully basting and flavouring it with his special blend of herbs. On the tables a magnificent array of gastronomic delights awaited. I sometimes think there is an unspoken competition among the women to produce the most mouth-watering food possible. If I'm right, I can only say it's great to be a beneficiary. There was a wonderful dish of lambs' kidneys and mushrooms, sweetbreads done in a kind of *beurre blanc*, fresh *mozzarelle* and *ricotta*, a deep-pan omelette, *pizza rustica*, stuffed aubergines, grilled peppers in strips marinated in olive oil and garlic, home-made *prosciutto* and *salsicce*, breads, salads and then, with a flourish, Cessidio's ember-cooked lamb. Everyone had brought their best wine. Graziano had brought the one that had won a prize the summer before at the wine-tasting, and, not to be outdone, so had Nicola. Diodato, who sells wine, brought wonderful full-bodied reds from the Abruzzi. It was a feast that could hold its own with previous years, but the greatest improvement was the choice of place.

No one was in a great hurry to move after the food, so we lounged in the shade drinking *nocino*, the *digestivo* made from walnuts which comes into its own after the sort of over-indulgence we had just participated in. Even the children had slowed up and for a little while you could hear the cicadas and the occasional cow-bell across the valley. The hour allotted for digestion passed dreamily, as we each reflected on our good fortune to have eaten so fine a meal in such good company. Then it was time to swim again. It was Diodato who first discovered that you could get in behind the waterfall on to a ledge and then dive through the curtain of water into the pool. My wife was the only woman to swim. It is tempting to conclude that Italian women have less sense of fun than their menfolk, preferring instead to sit on the banks and watch, rather than join in. It is true that the women we know are not much inclined to exercise, be it walking, sport or in this case swimming. It is also entirely possible that this is a local characteristic and not mirrored nationally, although I have noticed at the beach that the women tend to sunbathe rather than bathe.

Since the discovery of this mountain pool only twenty minutes from our house, summer days have been transformed. We no longer dread the build up of heat in August and there is pleasure in finding something in Italy that you don't have to pay through the nose for. On several occasions we have been enthralled by a pair of circling eagles overhead, riding thermals majestically. I'm hoping that the Italian predilection for fashion will not turn our river into the peopled mayhem of the swimming pools; we might just be saved by the belief held by many in our valley, that it can't be good or fashionable if it's free.